FROM ABSEN
ATTENDA

Alastair Evans is a senior lecturer in HRM at Thames Valley University, Ealing. He holds an MA in industrial relations from the University of Warwick and is a fellow of the CIPD. Prior to his current post, he was a HR director in the computer software industry and, before that, a HR consultant in the same industry. He also worked for the (former) Institute of Personnel Management as a policy adviser in the field of employee resourcing.

He has published more than a dozen books over the last 20 years on such topics as human resource planning, computerised HR systems, recruitment and retention, and flexible working patterns. Over the past five years, he has been published widely and has given numerous conference papers on absence and attendance management.

Mike Walters is a director of the consulting firm Whitmuir, specialising in HR strategy and business performance. His previous consulting career includes periods leading HR practices for both 'big 5' and specialist firms. Mike began his HR career with Shell and the BBC, and was also a policy adviser in employee resourcing issues with the then IPM. More recently, Mike was head of human resources development with the Co-operative Bank plc, leading the development and implementation of HR strategies to support the Bank's distinctive ethical positioning.

Mike is the author of a number of management books on such topics as culture change, employee attitude surveys, performance management and the management of change. Mike was educated at Queens' College, Cambridge, and subsequently gained post-graduate qualifications in HR management at the University of Westminster. He is a member of the CIPD.

Other titles in the series:

The Chartered Institute of Personnel and Development is the leading publisher of books and reports for personnel and training professionals, students, and for all those concerned with the effective management and development of people at work. For details of all our titles, please contact the Publishing Department:

tel. 020 8263 3387
fax 020 8263 3850
e-mail publish@cipd.co.uk
To view and purchase CIPD books, visit the online bookstore:
www.cipd.co.uk/bookstore

FROM ABSENCE TO ATTENDANCE

Second Edition

Alastair Evans
and
Mike Walters

Chartered Institute of Personnel and Development

First edition © Alastair Evans and Steve Palmer, 1997
First published in 1997
Reprinted 1999, 2000

Second edition © Alastair Evans and Mike Walters
This edition published in 2002
Reprinted 2003

Design by Paperweight
Typesetting by Intype London Ltd
Printed in Great Britain by The Cromwell Press,
Trowbridge, Wiltshire

British Library Cataloguing in Publication Data
A catalogue record for this book is available from the British Library

ISBN 0-85292-935-8

Chartered Institute of Personnel and Development. CIPD House,
Camp Road, London SW19 4UX
Tel: 020 8971 9000 Fax: 020 8263 3333
E-mail: cipd@cipd.co.uk Website: www.cipd.co.uk
Incorporated by Royal Charter. Registered charity no. 1079797

CONTENTS

ACKNOWLEDGEMENTS

We are most grateful to Steve Palmer, co-author of the first edition of this book, for allowing us to reuse some of his material in this edition. Alun Lewis, Chief Executive of James Cropper plc, and Grahame Ritchie, Head of Employee Resourcing at the Scottish Prison Service, kindly supplied information for the stimulating case studies about their organisations. And we would also like to thank the following for granting us permission to use copyright material: ACAS, Addison-Wesley publishers, Blackhall publishers, the CBI, Gee Publishing (a Thomson company), Industrial Relations Services, and the Institute of Employment Studies.

INTRODUCTION

Every working day, something like a million people in Britain are absent from work. Approaching 200 million days are lost each year through absence, excluding holidays and authorised leave, and the cost to the economy has been estimated at £12 billion. To an organisation employing 1,000 people on average salary scales, an annual absence rate of 5 per cent will translate into close to £1 million lost per year. Despite these high costs, the CIPD's (2001) absence survey found that a fifth of all organisations do not even bother to keep absence statistics and, according to IRS (1998) and Gee (1999), as many as three quarters or more have no idea of the cost of absence to them. Since these tasks are usually the responsibility of the human resource (HR) department, this apparent lack of concern for a major organisational cost is decidedly worrying.

The issue of absence has risen up the agenda of many organisations in the past few years. Three quarters of public-sector employers and over half of manufacturing employers now have specific targets for reducing absence. An important influence was the absence-reduction targets established by the Cabinet Office paper *Working Well Together*, requiring overall reductions in public-sector absence of 20 per cent by 2001 and 30 per cent by 2003. Further stimuli to the adoption of best practice in absence management and occupational health generally came from the launch in 2000 of the Health and Safety Commission's strategy documents *Revitalising Health and Safety* and *Securing Health Together*, which set a target of a 30 per cent reduction in days lost through work-related injury and ill health by 2010. Other pressures which have led employers to focus more closely on absence include (Bevan and Hayday, 1998):

☐ more stringent duties on employers under the law in relation to the physical and mental wellbeing of employees

☐ rising absence costs borne by employers as a result of changes in the statutory sick pay regulations

☐ the need to maintain and improve competitiveness, combined with a growing awareness of time lost through absence and its impact on productivity, efficiency and quality

☐ rising health awareness and expectations on the part of employees in relation to their mental and physical health at work.

The average national rate of absence represents around 8 to $8\frac{1}{2}$ days per employee per year. Yet there are, as we explain in detail in Chapter 1, wide variations by occupational group, region and size of firm. Manual workers lose on average around nine and a half days per year, while non-manuals lose about six and a half. Rates of absence in the public sector are on average 40 per cent higher than in the private sector, but even within the public sector absence performance varies widely. A top-performing government agency may lose only four days a year, while a poor performer loses more than three times as many. The story is much the same in the private sector, even though overall absence rates are lower. The best performers are found in construction, chemicals and professional services, where around two to two-and-a-half days are lost a year, whereas the food and drink industry loses up to five times as much. Yet even within the food and drink industry the best performers lose just four days per employee per year (CBI, 1997).

How can we explain such wide variation – two days lost per employee a year at one end of the scale and nearly a fortnight a year at the other? It is our contention that the difference lies in top management commitment to absence control, and in the implementation of appropriate policies and practices. HR practitioners can make a major contribution in bringing down the absence levels in organisations where they are unacceptably high, which soon means a significant impact on the cost line. Moreover, we see it as the task of HR professionals to benchmark and target best-practice performance levels, and to encourage a climate of continuous improvement.

Prevailing levels of absence need not be accepted as an inevitable fact of organisational life. High absence rates in such organisations as Oldham NHS Trust and the London Boroughs of Lewisham and Lambeth, sometimes running at 15 days or more per employee per year, have been reduced by half or more, and at the London Borough of Wandsworth – which started with lower absence rates than some other local authorities – absence has been cut by one third (Evans, 1999a, 2000a).

Examples of significant absence reduction have also been reported from the private sector. Connex railways cut absence rates by 40 per cent over four years (IDS, 2001), and at Vauxhall Motors rates have been reduced by a half or more over a period of years (Industrial Society, 2001). Equally impressive reductions have been reported in much smaller companies. At Walter Holland, a food manufacturer based in Accrington employing 500 people, absence has been halved from 11 to $5\frac{1}{2}$ per cent of time lost (IDS, 2001). Similarly at Wise Owl Publishing, employing 200 in Bristol, it was cut by half within a few months of commencing absence-reduction initiatives (Myland, 2000). At Tollitt & Harvey, a stationery manufacturer employing 170 in Kings Lynn, absence was cut from 8 per cent to around 2 per cent over two years (Arkin, 2001). Whereas methods varied, all the approaches used will be considered here.

This book is divided into two parts. The first looks at the challenge of absence. Chapter 1 examines the scale of the problem, and the need for timely data about time lost, frequency of absence, and costs. It also provides detailed statistical information on current absence levels so that employers can benchmark themselves against organisations comparable in size, region or industrial sector. Chapter 2 explores what we now know about the nature and different causes of absence. Chapter 3 sets out the many varied initiatives that organisations have adopted in response – both 'sticks' to discourage absence and 'carrots' to encourage attendance. Chapter 4 provides guidance on the disciplinary and legal framework of absence management, such as the considerable body of case law which sets now fairly exacting standards for employers who, for example, want to dismiss long-term sick employees.

The second part of the book pulls all this together into a systematic and practical framework for the management of attendance. It demonstrates how managers can measure the impact of absence within their own organisations, ascertain the specific causes, and use this information to build an effective absence-control programme. The first of two Appendices highlights some of the key messages in case studies of effective absence management in action at James Cropper plc and the Scottish Prison Service. Appendix 2 provides a short directory of suppliers of materials for absence management training programmes.

PART I

THE CHALLENGE OF ABSENCE

1 MEASURING, MONITORING AND BENCHMARKING

The first step in controlling absence (or managing attendance) is measurement. Without this it is impossible to know what absence problem there is, if any, or to determine the most appropriate method for dealing with it. As noted in the Introduction, a significant minority of around a fifth of employers have no idea what levels of absence they have, and a significant majority of around three quarters have no idea what absence costs their organisation. As noted in the Introduction too, absence costs can be significant and costing absence – including measuring cost reductions achieved by bringing current levels down – provides the HR specialist with an important opportunity to demonstrate the impact of his or her initiatives on the bottom line.

This chapter is concerned with four aspects of measurement. Firstly, how is absence measured? Secondly, how much does absence cost, and how can we go about costing it in our organisations? Thirdly, how is absence monitored, and what practices are followed by organisations? Fourthly, how do absence levels in our organisation compare with the experience of similar organisations or more generally in the country as a whole? In this final section of the chapter we present a summary of the current statistics from a range of survey sources that will enable organisations to benchmark current absence levels in a variety of different ways. Surveys show that different absence levels apply by organisation size, sector, occupational group, regional location, etc, so different sets of benchmark data may needed in order to carry out adequate comparisons.

Measuring absence

A number of ways to measure absence are considered in this section:

- □ time lost measures
- □ frequency measures
- □ 'Bradford factor' measures
- □ other formulae for measurement.

Time lost measures

The most common method of measuring sickness absence is to calculate the number of lost days/shifts as a proportion of the potential total number of days/shifts worked. This has been termed a 'time lost measure' and is the approach adopted in most organisations and also by the CBI in its national surveys of sickness absence. The CBI asks respondents for their absence rate assuming a 228-day working year (ie 365 minus weekends, eight public holidays and 25 days' annual leave). Although this approach is common, however, it is also rather crude and raises some problems. If you are bench-marking against other organisations, it is not possible to be certain whether their base calculation – or even their defi-nition of absence – is the same. Some organisations use a 365-day year, for instance, while others include annual leave; and because it measures lost time in total, this index tends to over-emphasise long-term sickness in the absence statistics. 'Days' may not be the most appropriate measure of time anyway. For part-time employees, for example, hours lost may be better. Despite these difficulties, the time lost measure is the most important for benchmarking purposes because it is the one used in all the published surveys which normally express time lost in terms of a percentage and an average number of days. The time lost measure can also be used to analyse absence within an organisation by occupational group, department, location, etc.

ACAS (1999) expresses the time lost formula as:

$$\frac{\text{Total absence (hours or days) in the period}}{\text{Possible total (hours or days) in the period}} \times 100$$

So, for example, if the total absence in the period is 124 person-hours and the total time available is 1,550 person-hours, the lost time rate is:

$$\frac{124}{1,550} \times 100$$

$$= 8 \text{ per cent}$$

In order to calculate time lost in terms of average days per employee, the formula is:

$$\frac{\text{Total time lost in the period (in days)}}{\text{Average number of employees employed in the period}} \times 100$$

Using the data from the above example, if 50 people on average were employed in the period, the calculation would be:

$$\frac{124 \text{ hours lost in period}}{\text{Average of 50 employed in period}}$$

$$= 2.4 \text{ days per employee}$$

When making the above calculation, it is important to take account of part-time working. If, in the above example, 10 of the 50 employees were part-timers who all worked half the standard week, it would then be necessary to count employees in terms of 'full-time equivalents' (FTEs). In the above example, the full-time equivalent figure would be 45 and the average days lost would be 2.8 days per employee.

A further difficulty exists with this formula – as pointed out by the BMI (1998) in its analysis of civil service absence data – which leads to an undercalculation of the true level of absence. Company absence statistics usually assume that each employee is available for work for a whole working year, but this is not so in the case of any employee who has joined and left during the year. For example, an employee who has joined and left within a three-month period may also have taken two days absent. Most absence statistics would count this as two days lost in a year, but in reality this is the equivalent of eight days lost on an annualised basis. The authors of the BMI (1998) report advocate the use of the concept of a 'staff year' to correct the undercalculation. This involves identifying the number of working days in a full year, less weekends (if not normally worked), bank holidays and average holiday entitlement. In the case of the civil service this constitutes 225 working days. Where staff have been employed throughout the year, their absence is calculated on this basis. Where staff have been employed for less than a year, their absences in the period worked are recalculated on an annualised basis. The authors conclude that the staff year adjustment provides a more reliable measure of average absence figures than simply a count of staff employed. The formula for readjusting absence days on an annualised basis for each employee who has worked for less than a full year is:

$$\frac{\text{Number of days actually lost in a period}}{\text{Number of working days available in a period}} \times 225$$

In the case of someone who had lost 10 days in a period of employment lasting three months, and assuming that the average number of working days was a quarter of 225 (ie 56.25), this calculation would be:

$$\frac{10 \text{ days lost}}{56.25 \text{ days available}} \times 225$$

$$= 40 \text{ days (annualised equivalent)}$$

Frequency measures

Another approach measures the frequency of absence – that is, the number of separate absence spells. ACAS (1999) suggests two formulae. The first, the 'frequency rate', measures the average number of spells of absence per employee and is particularly helpful in determining whether time lost is due to lots of short absences or a few long absences. The frequency rate is calculated by the formula:

$$\frac{\text{Number of spells of absence in the period}}{\text{Number employed in the period}} \times 100$$

So, for example, if in a period 80 people were employed and 12 had been away absent, one away three times, two away twice, and nine more away once, a total of 16 spells of absence would have been incurred, and the frequency-rate calculation would be:

$$\frac{16 \text{ absence spells in period}}{\text{Total of 80 employed in period}} \times 100$$

$$= 20 \text{ per cent}$$

Frequency rates highlight the number of spells so that percentages will be higher where there are frequent short absences and lower where absence consists mainly of few employees who have longer-term absences.

An alternative formula is the 'individual frequency rate', also known as the 'incidence' or 'prevalence rate', which shows the proportion of the workforce who have incurred any absence during a period. This formula is:

$$\frac{\text{Number of employees having one or more spells of absence in a period}}{\text{Total number employed in a period}} \times 100$$

In the above example 12 employees were absent in the period, and the calculation would be:

$$\frac{12 \text{ employees with at least one spell of absence}}{\text{A total of 80 employed}} \times 100$$

In effect, the formula is stating that 15 per cent of the workforce incurred at least one absence, whereas 85 per cent had a full attendance record.

'Bradford factor' measures

Because short-term absences can be more disruptive, a frequency index may be a better measure of the overall impact of absence on an organisation than purely total time lost. It also lends itself to weighting through analyses such as the 'Bradford factor', an approach devised at the University of Bradford. The approach focuses attention on the frequency of an individual's absence by awarding points in a weighted way which emphasises spells of absence. The full equation is:

$$\text{Points scored} = (S \times S) \times D$$

where S is the number of spells of absence over a period (typically 12 months) and D equals total days off in the same period. If frequency of absence is the major issue, the Bradford approach allows policies to be triggered on this basis rather than the more normal 'so many days in so many months'. For example, one absence of five days would be awarded, say, 5 points – $(1 \times 1) \times 5$ – but five absences of one day would receive 125 points – $(5 \times 5) \times 5$. We consider trigger points in more detail in Chapter 3.

The problem is that although a Bradford-type measure is better for deciding what policies to adopt and when to implement different stages, for the purposes of benchmarking we have to accept that most organisations use a pure time-lost measure. Organisations might therefore find it helpful to use a time-lost measure for general external comparisons, but a frequency-based measure to help design their internal personnel approach to absence management.

Other measures

A further range of formulae are also available for measuring absence, and some of them are considered in this section. CCH (2000) suggests that measures of absence inception – ie measures of absences starting in a period – may be useful for monitoring purposes. For example, calculating these figures on a monthly basis can be used to show whether absences are stable or not, and to establish whether more spells of absence have started in a period or whether more staff have started absence spells in the period. The formulae for measuring 'inception rates' for spells of absence starting in a period is:

$$\frac{\text{Number of spells of absence starting in a period}}{\text{Average number of staff employed in a period}} \times 100$$

The formula for calculating the inception rate for individuals starting an absence in a period is:

$$\frac{\text{Number starting at least one spell of absence in a period}}{\text{Average number of staff employed in a period}} \times 100$$

CCH (1997b) also offers a couple of formulae for calculating the duration of absences. The average duration per spell is given by the formula:

$$\frac{\text{Total duration of all spells ending during a period}}{\text{Number of spells ending in the period}}$$

The average duration per person is calculated by:

$$\frac{\text{Total time lost from spells ending in the period}}{\text{Number of staff having an absence in the period}}$$

Costing absence

A good way to convince senior management that absence ought to be tackled, and to justify to them the need for investment in, for example, computerisation to help monitor absence levels, is to show them the figures. Costing absence is comparatively simple, especially if the focus is just on the *direct* wage costs – ie the cost of paying employees off sick. Calculating other related absence costs is more difficult, but it may be possible to include some other costs if known – for example, costs of temporary replacements or additional overtime working – but more indirect costs can require some subjective judgements. How, for instance, can reduced quality of service or poorer customer care be measured in financial terms, at least in the shorter term? In the CBI's (2001) absence survey, two thirds of respondents were able to quantify direct costs, but only 5 per cent felt able to provide an estimate of indirect costs.

A useful *pro forma* for calculating the direct wage costs of absence has been provided by Hugo Fair (1992):

Sample form for calculation

Cost of absenteeism

Enter number of employees	_____ (a)	
Enter average weekly wage	£_____ (b)	
Multiply (a) × (b)	£_____ (c)	
Multiply (c) × 52	£_____	= total paybill
Enter total absence days per year	_____ (d)	
Enter total number working days per year	_____ (e)	
Divide [(d) × 100] by [(a) × (e)]	_____% (f)	absence rate
Multiply (b)/5 × (d)	£_____ (g)	= absence cost per year

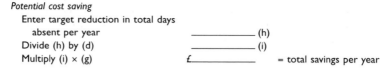

Source: Personnel and Profit. London, IPM

Using the above form for an organisation with 500 employees, with average earnings of £400 per week, an average working year of 228 days per employee, and an absence level of 10 days per employee per year, we can calculate that the annual direct cost of absence is £400,000. A reduction in the absence level from 10 to eight days would save £80,000 a year. This data could be produced on a disaggregated basis by establishments, departments or workgroups, if necessary. The full worked example using the above form is as follows:

Cost of absenteeism

Enter number of employees	500	(a)
Enter average weekly wage	£400	(b)
Multiply (a) × (b)	£200,000	(c)
Multiply (c) × 52	£10,400,000	= total paybill
Enter total absence days per year	5,000	(d)
Enter total number working days per year	228	(e)
Divide [(d) ×100] by [(a) × (e)]	4.39%	(f) = absence rate
Multiply (b)/5 × (d)	£400,000	(g) = absence cost per year

Potential cost saving

Enter target reduction in total days absent per year	100 days	(h)
Divide (h) by (d)	0.2	(i)
Multiply (i) × (g)	£80,000	= total savings per year

Information on the costs of absence to UK organisations is provided by the CBI and CIPD annual absence surveys. The CIPD (2001) put the average cost at £487 per employee per year, making a total annual cost to the UK economy as a whole of £12 billion. The CBI (2001) put the direct cost at £434 per employee per year, a figure which has remained broadly the same over the last few years. Projected across the whole workforce, the total cost would be £10.7 billion. The CBI (2001) also broke down annual costs per employee by broad sector:

- □ public   £482
- □ private   £432
- □ manufacturing   £461
- □ services   £425.

The CIPD (2000) provided the following more detailed breakdown of direct costs per employee per annum, in rank order by sector:

health	£741
chemicals	£695
paper and printing	£691
other public services	£613
transport, storage and communications	£545
finance	£538
local government	£533
central government	£527
mining and quarrying	£521
general services	£488
electricity, gas and water	£474
engineering and metals	£451
general manufacturing	£409
textiles	£384
food, drink and tobacco	£368
retail and wholesale	£305
hotel, restaurants and leisure	£291
construction	£276

Something of a debate has emerged about the extent to which these figures represent the real direct costs of absence. Some doubt was cast by the CIPD (2001) absence survey on the accuracy of absence recording and reporting in organisations. According to respondents to the CIPD (2001) survey, underreporting by managers of their own absences could be as high as 95 per cent of actual time lost in some organisations. Across all respondents, one third believed that managers do underreport their own absence, and the average estimate of this underreporting was 27 per cent of actual time lost.

A second issue relates to the basis upon which organisations provide survey enquiries with estimates of the direct costs of absence. According to Gee (1999), two thirds of employers base the cost on the salary or company sick pay of the absent employee, whereas just over one third take into account the costs of additional overtime, lost time and lost productivity. In the CBI's annual absence surveys, respondents are asked to base their calculations of direct absence costs on the salary costs of absent employees, replacement costs (ie temporary staff or additional overtime) and lost service or production time (CBI, 2001), but in the light of the Gee findings there may be a question about whether respondents have reliable information about the additional cost aspects asked about. The overall conclusion seems to be that estimates of the direct costs of absence may be understated.

A third issue to emerge from estimates of absence costs relates to the difficult question of estimating indirect costs. The CBI's annual absence surveys have endeavoured to gather information about this by asking respondents to provide an estimate of them, including the costs of lowered customer service or poorer quality of products or services leading to a loss of future business (CBI, 2001). As the CBI note (p.16), these costs are difficult for employers to estimate and the question has tended to generate a low response rate in their surveys. The results obtained to their question about indirect absence costs between 1998 and 2001 have been highly variable, ranging from the same again as direct costs (CBI, 2001), to one and a half times direct costs (CBI, 1998), to almost double direct costs (CBI, 2000), to as much as four times direct costs (CBI, 2000). Taking the mid-range figure for 1998 which indicated that indirect absence costs were double direct costs, the total annual cost per employee in that year was £1,348, made up of direct costs of £478 and indirect costs of £870. Another survey from Watson Wyatt in 1998 (in CCH, 1999) put the total annual cost per employee of short absence alone considerably higher at £1,900. Based on an average of eight days lost per employee per year, the total was made up of the direct cost of salaries and benefits of £700 and the indirect costs of employing cover and other inefficiencies at £1,200. As regards the costs of long-term sickness, Watson Wyatt estimated that a further 1 to 2 per cent of payroll costs had to be added to the costs of short-term absence. More recently, research from the Institute of Employment Studies (Bevan and Hayday, 2001; Bevan, 2001) has endeavoured to explore the issue of absence costs in more depth using a case study approach. Bevan and Hayday (2001) broke the costs of absence into three categories – direct costs, indirect costs and management costs – although it might be noted that the indirect costs did not include such elements as impact on workforce morale, product and service quality, productivity, customer retention, or other negative business outcomes. The cost elements contained in each of the three categories used by Bevan and Hayday (2001) were:

☐ direct costs of salary and benefits – annual salary, employer's National Insurance contributions, employer's pension contributions, bonus payments, contracted over-time, car allowances, private healthcare, disability (or permanent health) insurance cover and any other benefits

☐ indirect costs – the costs of internal replacement workers (overtime and 'acting up' payments) and the costs of external replacement workers in terms of daily agency costs

☐ management costs incurred by absence – line manager time and costs in relation to arranging cover, conducting return-to-work interviews, supervising replacements and other absence administration; HR departments' costs in terms of the time taken to collate and report on absence data and carry out other absence administration; the costs of training department time spent training line managers in absence management; and the costs of health pro-motion, including employee assistance programmes, subsidised facilities relating to health awareness/pro-motion and occupational health services.

Bevan and Hayday's (2001) summarised list of total absence costs taking into account all the costs elements identified is as shown in Table 1:

Table I **ABSENCE COSTS**

Organisation	Absence rate (%)	Absence costs as percentage of paybill	Average annual cost per employee (£)
Retail company			
Small store	8.1	11.2	861
Medium store	4.0	6.8	465
Large store	7.5	16.4	1,268
Insurance company	2.4	4.7	991
Financial services company	3.2	7.8	1,677
Local authority	4.2	8.2	2,261
Regulatory body	1.9	2.2	809
Retail group	5.2	6.5	497
Department in law firm	1.3	1.8	837
AVERAGE	4.2	7.3	1,074

Source: S. Bevan and S. Hayday (2001) *Costing Sickness Absence in the UK*. Institute for Employment Studies. page 44

Overall, the average annual cost of absence varied from £465 in a medium store to £2,261 in a local authority. The survey also identified elsewhere that the proportion of total costs accounted for by long-term absence varied between 30 and 70 per cent of all absence costs, and that a high prevalence of long-term sickness absence was likely to push total absence costs up. Overall, the survey found that at an average rate of just over 4 per cent absence across the sample organisations – slightly above the national average – absence costs worked out on average at a little above 7 per cent of total payroll costs. Such a cost might provide a useful yardstick for costing the impact of both direct and indirect absences in organisations where absences are close to the national average, although it should be noted that the actual experience of organisations in the sample showed that costs varied from under 2 per cent to over 16 per cent of payroll.

Monitoring absence

Surveys suggest that absence is monitored through a combination of computerised and manual recording systems. The CIPD (2000) absence survey found that 80 per cent of organisations had a computerised absence-recording system and 60 per cent recorded at least some data manually. The survey also showed, perhaps not surprisingly, that computerisation increased by organisation size, around 60 per cent of organisations of less than 100 employees having access to a computerised record, compared to 85 per cent or more of organisations which employed 500 or above. Gee (1999) found lower levels of use of computerised absence records at around 50 per cent of organisations employing 500 or more, and the CIPD (2001) finding may indicate some increase in the use of computers in this area. The respondents to the Gee (1999) survey were also asked about a number of possible uses of absence records, and the responses were:

☐ as part of the individual employee record (95 per cent)
☐ for payroll and sick-pay calculations (90 per cent)
☐ to trigger disciplinary measures relating to absence (80 per cent)
☐ to generate departmental/organisational attendance figures (70 per cent)
☐ to determine attendance bonuses (15 per cent).

In relation to the responsibility for entering absence data, Gee (1999) found that in over a third of organisations this lay with the HR department; in under a third it was the responsibility of the line manager; and in around a fifth it was the responsibility of both HR and the line. The survey also found that in 8 per cent of organisations employees themselves were responsible for entering the data, a trend which may since have grown as a result of the more widespread use of company intranets. As regards the type of absence-monitoring reports produced, the following responses were given:

☐ analysis of days lost (95 per cent)
☐ analysis of absence by department/group (70 per cent)
☐ analysis of absence by cause (45 per cent)
☐ analysis of absence costs (38 per cent)
☐ analysis of absence by grade/job category (30 per cent).

IRS (1998) explored in a survey the frequency with which absence reports were generated and to whom they were sent. A total of 60 per cent of organisations produced monthly absence reports, 15 per cent produced them quarterly, under 10 per cent produced them weekly, and a similar percentage said that they never produced absence reports. The main recipients of absence reports in two thirds or more organisations were line or departmental managers, but in half the organisations surveyed absence reports also went to the board of directors, in a third to supervisors and in 13 per cent to staff representatives.

It is also important to remember that the role of the computer in absence management goes beyond the production of management information, important though that is, to encompass the automation of absence administration, as was pointed out by Evans (1999b). For a range of absence-control policies to be effective it is important that the software is capable of generating reminders for action on the part of the HR function or line managers, without which the required actions may not be implemented. The effectiveness of such policies as using return-to-work interviews or 'trigger-points' requiring action after some threshold of absence has been met or exceeded, perhaps requiring an absence-review meeting or disciplinary action, may be dependent on reminding those who need to know that some action is required. From another perspective, the role of the computer is increasingly being integrated into time and attendance systems which automatically record an employee's attendance or absence, thus reducing the need for any manual entry of absence data at all.

Benchmarking your organisation

Benchmarking is important because it provides information on how well an organisation is performing against competitors and the world at large, highlighting areas for improvement, and helping to set performance standards.

Prior to the early 1990s, when the CBI commenced its current series of absence surveys, the main sources of information about absence trends came from the government's General Household Survey and later its Labour Force Survey – and the latter remains a relevant source. Since the early 1990s, an abundance of both qualitative and quantitative survey data has been published which, in particular, has provided many insights into absence-management practices rarely generated before. In addition to the series of annual absence surveys provided by the CBI (CBI, 1993, 1995–2001), the CIPD commenced an annual series in 2000 (see CIPD, 2000, 2001), and periodic surveys have also been produced by the Industrial Society (1994, 1997, 2000, 2001), by Industrial Relations Services in its *Employment Review* (see IRS, 1994, 1998), the Institute of Employment Studies (Bevan and Hayday, 1998) and Gee (1999). Taken together, these surveys provide extensive information about, for example, absence by organisation size, industrial sector, region, occupational group, and so on, and also generate a good deal of useful information about trends in the absence-management practices of organisations.

When using published survey data for benchmarking purposes, it is first important to note that the majority of respondents to the CBI and CIPD surveys are from smaller organisations which tend to have lower levels of absence than larger organisations. In the CBI and CIPD's absence surveys for 2001, for example, nearly 60 per cent of respondents were from organisations (or workplaces) of less than 500 employees – so larger organisations must be cautious when comparing themselves to overall averages where the size of organisations has not been specified.

Secondly, some of the data from these sources can be very volatile over time and sometimes relate to small sample sizes less representative when the data are disaggregated. For example, comparing the CBI regional and industrial data for the last few years shows considerable movement in the ranking order of the best and worst performers. Often this results from the very low sample sizes in some sectors and regions which can distort the results from year to year. It is possible to have reasonable confidence in the broader figures, and in the more general occupational and industrial data. Otherwise, it would be sensible to look at benchmarking data over a period of years to check whether there has been a lot of volatility and to decide how much faith should be attached to them.

When benchmarking data that meets an individual organisation's needs has been located, it is important to remember that no target should be set just to get an organisation's absence rate to the average. The CBI statistics give some limited absence data by average and quartile, and the data for 2001 shows that employers in the worst-performing upper quartile can experience more than twice as much absence as employers at the best-performing lower quartile. Getting to the average might be an immediate objective, but being amongst the best 25 per cent makes a better longer-term aim and will help to keep managing absence firmly on your organisation's agenda.

The remainder of this chapter brings together all the current or more recently available statistics for benchmarking absence. It is important to note that the various sources referred to use differing methodologies for gathering data, have differing sample sizes, and were also published at different dates. Percentages of working time lost or days lost therefore vary between the tables according to the source and the year of collection.

Trends in time lost: 1990–2000

Table 2 **TRENDS IN ABSENCE LEVELS 1990–2000, AS % OF TOTAL WORKING TIME**

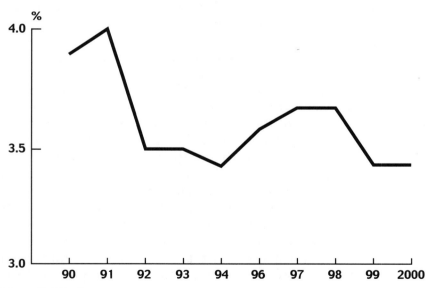

Source: CBI, 2001. p.10

Table 2 shows that absence levels at the beginning of the decade ran at about 4 per cent of working time lost, and fell to around 3.5 per cent during the recessionary years of the earlier 1990s, before rising again. It remains to be seen whether the apparent downward trend emerging at the end of the period will continue. The average level of absence stood at 3.6 per cent and overall rates remained fairly stable, showing only small deviations either side in each year's results.

Average days lost and percentage of time lost by quartile across the UK: 1999 and 2000

Table 3 ABSENCE LEVELS ACROSS THE UNITED KINGDOM

Year	All respondents		Best performing quartile		Worst performing quartile	
	Average days lost	% of working time	Average days lost	% of working time	Average days lost	% of working time
2000	7.8	3.4	4.6	2.0	10.0	4.4
1999	7.8	3.4	5.3	2.3	10.4	3.7

Source: CBI, 2001. p.11

Table 3 shows the wide difference in performance between the best- and worst-performing quartiles in 2000. The worst-performing organisations (at 10 days lost on average per employee) incur around double the absence of the best performers (4.6 days), and a gap of 5.4 days per employee yawns between the two. The implications are that organisations which wish to target absence levels against the best performers should aim for an average absence per employee of five days or less per year.

Absence levels for manual and non-manual employees by quartile across the UK: 1999 and 2000

Table 4 shows that manual employee absence is – as is usually to be expected – higher than non-manual, although the CBI notes that manual worker absence has been falling

Table 4 ABSENCE LEVELS FOR MANUAL AND NON-MANUAL EMPLOYEES
(% of working time in brackets)

Employees	Average in 2000	Best performing quartile	Median quartile	Worst performing quartile	Average in 1999
Manual	9.5 (4.2)	5.5 (2.4)	9.0 (3.9)	12.1 (5.3)	9.2 (4.0)
Non-manual	6.3 (2.8)	3.5 (1.5)	5.3 (2.3)	8.6 (3.8)	6.5 (2.8)

Source: CBI, 2001. p.11

over the longer term. Again, the table shows that the worst-performing sectors in relation to both manual and non-manual workers experience more than twice as much time lost through absence compared to the best performers. The figures suggest that when benchmarking and setting targets against the best-performing sectors, organisations should aim for five to six days lost per year for manual workers, and three to four days among non-manuals.

Absence by broad sector: 1999 and 2000

Table 5 ABSENCE LEVELS BY BROAD SECTOR

Sector	Number of working days lost (all employees)	
	2000	1999
Public	10.2	9.9
Private	7.2	7.1
– manufacturing	6.9	8.0
– services	7.7	7.0

Source: CBI, 2001. p.12

Table 5 shows that absence is higher in the public sector than in the private sector, the former incurring around 40 per cent more days lost in 2000. It also indicates a slightly widening gap between public- and private-sector absence in 2000 compared to 1999. For benchmarking purposes, public-sector organisations achieving less than 10 days lost per employee per year – or private-sector companies beating 7 days per year – will be performing better than average for their sector.

Absence by sector: 2000

Table 6 **AVERAGE LEVEL OF SICKNESS ABSENCE BY SECTOR**

Main sector	Average % of working time lost	Average days lost per employee per year
Food, drink and tobacco (n=78)	5.0	11.4
Health (n=85)	4.8	10.9
Local government (n=83)	4.8	10.9
Textiles (n=19)	4.2	9.6
Central government (n=37)	4.2	9.6
Other public services (n=35)	4.0	9.1
General manufacturing (n=217)	3.9	8.9
Transport, storage and communications (n=60)	3.9	8.9
Other private sector (n=63)	3.9	8.9
Engineering and metals (n=112)	3.7	8.4
Mining and quarrying (n=2)	3.7	8.4
Education (n=64)	3.6	8.2
Defence activities (n=4)	3.6	8.2
Retail and wholesale (n=70)	3.4	7.7
Paper and printing (n=30)	3.1	7.1
Chemicals (n=23)	3.0	6.8
General services (n=75)	2.9	6.6
Hotels, restaurants and leisure (n=25)	2.9	6.6
Finance (n=79)	2.7	6.2
Electricity, gas and water (n=17)	2.5	5.7
Agriculture and forestry (n=4)	2.1	4.8
Construction (n=23)	2.1	4.8
Survey average	**3.8**	**8.7**

Source: CIPD, 2001. p.5

The CIPD survey provides a detailed breakdown of average time lost and average days lost by 22 sectors of the economy in descending order of performance, although response rates from sectors is low and should be treated with caution. Table 6 shows a wide range of differences between sectors, the worst performers – such as food, drink and tobacco, health and local government – experiencing more than double the levels of absence compared to the best-performing sectors, such as agriculture and construction. Organisations may wish to use this data to set targets so as to at least match, if not improve upon, the average days lost per year in their sector.

Absence by workforce size

Table 7 **AVERAGE LEVEL OF SICKNESS ABSENCE BY WORKFORCE SIZE**

Workforce size	Average % of working time lost	Average days lost per employee per year
1–99 (n=78)	2.2	5.0
100–249 (n=260)	3.2	7.3
250–499 (n=315)	3.8	8.7
500–749 (n=160)	4.1	9.3
750–999 (n=86)	4.9	11.2
1000–1499 (n=85)	4.3	9.8
1500–1999 (n=31)	3.7	8.4
2000 and over (n=185)	4.5	10.3
Survey average	**3.8**	**8.7**

Source: CIPD, 2001. p.6

As has often been found in analyses of absence by organisation or workforce size, absence tends to rise as organisation size increases, such that organisations of over 2,000 employees incur twice as much time lost per employee than in the smallest organisations. Yet, as can be seen from the data in Table 7, the correlation between absence and organisation size is not a perfect one, and – as noted by the CIPD survey – other influences, such the age profile of a workforce, may intervene in the relationship between absence and organ-isation size. Organisations may wish to use this data by size to set targets for achieving or improving upon the benchmark averages for organisations of a comparable size.

Absence by region

Table 8 **AVERAGE LEVEL OF SICKNESS ABSENCE BY REGION**

Region*	Average % of working time lost	Average days lost per employee per year
North East (n=133)	4.2	9.6
North West (n=166)	4.2	9.6
Wales (n=47)	4.2	9.6
Midlands (n=186)	4.1	9.3
East Anglia (n=73)	3.9	8.9
South West (n=92)	3.9	8.9
Scotland (n=85)	3.6	8.2
South East (n=295)	3.4	7.7
Nationwide (n=185)	3.2	7.3
Northern Ireland (n=1)	3.0	6.8
Survey average	**3.8**	**8.7**

*Respondents were asked to indicate the main region to which their responses apply.
Source: CIPD, 2001

The analysis of absence by region in Table 8 shows that the north of England and Wales incurred higher absence levels, whereas the South-East was the only region to have below-national-average absence rates (discounting Northern Ireland, which had only one respondent). It is important to note, however, that regional analyses vary considerably over time and between different surveys. The CBI's results for 2001, for example, showed that the North-East and Wales had among the lowest rates of absence in the UK for non-manual workers, whereas Greater London had the highest rate of manual worker absence. It is also important to remember that regional statistics reflect their industrial and employment structures, so that a prevalence of manual working tends to push up average absence rates. Although regional absence data present difficulties for benchmarking purposes because of their fluctuations over time, organisations may wish to take regional factors into account when setting absence-reduction targets.

Absence by broad occupational group

Table 9   SICKNESS ABENCE BY OCCUPATIONAL GROUP

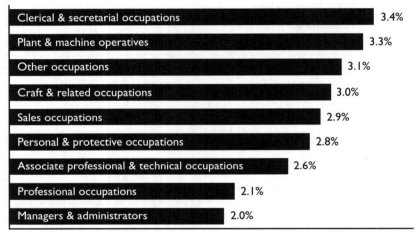

Percentage of employees off work through sickness or injury in reference week

Occupation	Percentage
Clerical & secretarial occupations	3.4%
Plant & machine operatives	3.3%
Other occupations	3.1%
Craft & related occupations	3.0%
Sales occupations	2.9%
Personal & protective occupations	2.8%
Associate professional & technical occupations	2.6%
Professional occupations	2.1%
Managers & administrators	2.0%

Source: Office for National Statistics (Labour Force Survey, summer 2000)

Beyond dividing absence into manual and non-manual groups, neither the CBI nor the CIPD survey provides analysis of absence by occupational group. Occupational analyses of absence are provided by the government's Office for National Statistics in its Labour Force Survey, and Table 9 shows the results for Summer 2000. The general picture is that absence declines with seniority of position, although perhaps surprisingly (given generally lower absence rates amongst non-manual staff) clerical and secretarial occupations incur more absence than any other occupational group. Since absence

levels vary considerably by broad occupational groups, organisations may wish to use these benchmarks when setting
targets for different groups of employees.

Proportions of absence: short- and long-term

Both the CBI and the CIPD reported on this in their 2001
surveys. Using a definition of short-term absence as being of
five days' duration or less, the CBI found that short-term
absences accounted for 62 per cent of time lost, while the
CIPD put the figure slightly lower at 55 per cent. The CIPD
also noted considerable sectoral variances, as much as 68 per
cent of time lost being accounted for by short-term absences
in finance, general services, leisure, retailing and wholesaling,
whereas in the public sector short-term absence accounted
for 46 per cent of total time lost. In terms of absence incidences or spells, the CBI found not surprisingly that short-
term absences accounted for 80 per cent of total incidences,
the remaining 20 per cent being accounted for by long-term
absence spells.

Absence across European countries

Absence rates across Europe are not collated on a regular or
systematic basis, but the figures were collected on a one-off
basis in research conducted by Grundemann and van Vuuren
(1998) for the European Foundation for the Improvement of
Living and Working Conditions and also reported by the CBI
(1999, p.20). The results obtained are shown in Table 10.

On both measures of absence, as indicated in Table 10, the
UK absence levels compared favourably with those of most
of the other countries for which data were available, ranking
second after Denmark in terms of percentage of working time
lost and second after Ireland in terms of time lost through
long-term absence. Considerable caution is required,
however, when interpreting these comparative figures since
the definition of what constitutes an absence can vary considerably from country to country. In a number of countries
the official figures are based on statutory sick pay entitlement
and exclude any unpaid waiting days. In Denmark, for
example, the first two weeks of absence are excluded because

Table 10 **LEVELS OF ABSENCE IN THE EU, 1998**

	Short-term absence rate	Long-term absence rate
Denmark	3.5	9.1
UK	3.6	5.5
Austria	4.1	
Sweden	4.4	12.7
Ireland	4.5	3.0
Norway	5.0	10.4
Netherlands	5.5	13.3
France	5.6	11.1
Germany	5.6	6.5
Belgium	5.8	6.6
Italy	6.9	5.7
Portugal	8.0	11.2

% of working time

Source: Grundemann and van Vuuren, 1998; CBI, 1999. p.20

sick pay costs in this period of absence are met by the employer. In Finland the first nine waiting days are not counted. In Portugal, by contrast, all absences for whatever reason are counted, and these are thought to account for about a quarter of the total.

Conclusion

This chapter has stressed the importance of measuring, costing, monitoring and benchmarking data. Together these procedures set the framework for managing absence. *Measuring* helps an organisation understand the nature of its absenteeism; *costing* quantifies its impact on the bottom line and the potential savings to be achieved from absence reductions; *monitoring* ensures that there is up-to-date information on where absence rates are going and is the foundation (as we shall see in Chapter 3) of many absence-control policies; and *benchmarking* provides information on where an organisation stands against comparators, and helps to set targets and objectives for an absence-management programme. Another ingredient in effective policy design is *understanding the causes* of absence and their relevance to explaining absence in your organisation. We look at causes in the next chapter.

2 THE CAUSES OF ABSENCE

Any effective programme of absence control has to start by analysing the causes of absence in order to devise the appropriate policies. As will be discussed further in Chapter 5, an organisation's absence records should provide some guidance on the reasons given, days lost, frequency and overall patterns by department, grade, occupational group or location. It must be recognised, however, that any analysis of the reasons given for absence will suffer from certain limitations. Quite evidently, the reason given for short-term, self-certificated absence may or may not reflect the real underlying causes. It may therefore be worth carrying out a survey of the opinions of managers and supervisors and, if felt appropriate, employees themselves, about the causes.

The purpose of this chapter is to provide a summary of the main causes of absence identified by the research. The chapter emphasises that the causes of absence in any given organisation are unlikely, in most circumstances, to be explained by any single factor. Attempts by researchers to identify major single explanations of absence have been unsuccessful, and current thinking sees its causes in terms of multiple factors, the influence of which vary according to the organisational context. The chapter groups the causes into three categories: the influence of the personal characteristics of employees themselves; the influence of the organisation's policies and practices, or lack of them; and the influence of factors external to the organisation. Where further investigation – such as a survey of managers or supervisors – is under consideration, the causes of absence described in this chapter should be assessed and those considered relevant to the specific organisational context should be explored further in the investigation.

Single-factor explanations of absence

Up to the late 1970s, much of the research into absence focused on trying to find a single factor to explain it. By implication, if the single factor causing absence from work could be identified, employers could tackle it through the implementation of the appropriate policies. According to Nicholson (1977), research had identified three main categories of causes of absence:

☐ pain avoidance

☐ adjustment to work

☐ economic decision-making by employees.

Pain avoidance

The major cause of absence here is job dissatisfaction, and the resultant absence is marked by its frequency. In essence, employees who are dissatisfied with their jobs seek to avoid the consequent psychological 'pain' or tensions of this by staying away from their jobs more often. We now know, however, that job dissatisfaction cannot be seen as the single cause of absenteeism but is certainly one of a number of factors in the work situation that influence absenteeism.

Adjustment to work

The main thrust of this explanation is that absence is the result of the way employees adapt or adjust to the situation found in a new workplace. One way of looking at absence is to view it as part of the socialisation process by which an individual adopts the absence norms and culture which he or she finds in an unfamiliar workplace. New employees observe the absence behaviour of their colleagues and its consequences from the response of management. Where there appears to be tolerance of absenteeism involving little action from management, new employees tend to conform by adopting the absence norms of their work group. Although these ideas are not new and were first put forward over 40 years ago (Hill and Trist, 1953, 1955), there has been a recent revival in interest in absence cultures at the level of the work group, and we shall be returning to them later in this chapter.

Another 'adjustment to work' perspective sees absence in terms of an employee's response to both the intrinsic and the extrinsic rewards found in the workplace, and is associated with equity and exchange theory (Rhodes and Steers, 1990). In essence, this perspective argues that individuals expect a fair exchange between what they bring to their job in terms of their inputs of skills, knowledge, commitment and so on and the rewards or outcomes that they get out of it. These rewards may relate to intrinsic factors, such as job satisfaction, or extrinsic factors, such as pay and benefits. If individuals feel that there is some imbalance between their inputs and the outcomes, there is internal tension which they will seek to reduce. In this way, when individuals feel that either the intrinsic or extrinsic rewards fall short of their expectations, they will reduce the tension they may feel by putting less into the job. One possible response is to give the employer less of their time by going absent.

For management these ideas have several implications. First, if absence is seen by employees to be tolerated by management and carrying few consequences, employees are likely to adjust their absence behaviour accordingly. Moreover, employees expect fair rewards for their efforts, so both job satisfaction and the provision of pay and benefits perceived as fair must form part of any absence-control strategy.

Economic decision-making by employees

This group of ideas sees absence as the result of rational decisions made by employees on the basis of their assessment of the costs and benefits associated with absence. Where absence is associated with a cost (such as loss of pay), an individual may nevertheless go absent because he or she values the alternative (such as a day off) more. A fine summer's day may be too good to miss by going in to work! Such theories do not, however, explain why one employee may feel sufficient commitment to go in to work while another may stay away, but there has been research to support the view that the provision of occupational sick pay which either cushions or eliminates the economic cost of absence has led to higher levels of absenteeism – and this is a topic to which we shall return.

Integrated multiple-factor explanations of absence

More recent research has tended to emphasise the complex nature of the factors influencing absence and is associated in particular with the ideas of Nicholson (1977), Steers and Rhodes (1978, 1984) and Rhodes and Steers (1990). The implication of much of the earlier research was that absence was avoidable as long as its cause could be pinned down and the appropriate policies applied. Yet this did not explain how one employee might have a good attendance record while another might have a poor one. Explanations of absence behaviour had instead, it was argued, to take into account variations in the personal characteristics, attitudes, values and backgrounds of individuals. Moreover, otherwise motivated employees sometimes experienced constraints in their ability to attend. People did become genuinely ill and also got into domestic difficulties from time to time which prevented their attendance. As well as to enquire into why employees go absent, it was held to be equally pertinent to consider what factors influenced their attendance and what factors might prevent it. More recent explanations of absence thus take into account both absence and its converse, attendance.

One approach which takes into account factors influencing both absence and attendance is put forward by Nicholson (1977) and is illustrated in Figure 1. Nicholson starts from the not unreasonable assumption that attendance is normal behaviour, arguing that 'most people, most of the time, are on 'automatic pilot' to attend regularly, and that the search for the causes of absence is a search for those factors that disturb the regularity of attendance' (Nicholson, 1977, p.242). Whether they actually attend in a specific set of circumstances depends on a number of variables. The key variables are those that affect 'attachment and attendance motivation', each of which is influenced by a 'contextual factor'. Firstly, the personal characteristics of individuals – such as age or gender – influence absence. For example, older workers are likely to take more time off through sickness. Secondly,

Figure I **NICHOLSON'S MODEL OF ATTENDANCE MOTIVATION**

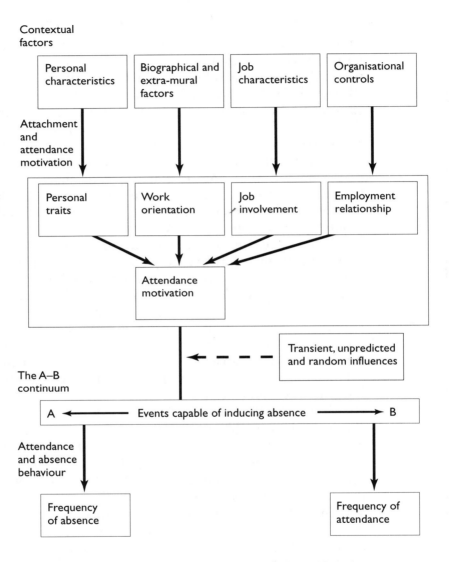

Contextual
factors

| Personal characteristics | Biographical and extra-mural factors | Job characteristics | Organisational controls |

Attachment
and
attendance
motivation

| Personal traits | Work orientation | Job involvement | Employment relationship |

Attendance
motivation

Transient, unpredicted
and random influences

The A–B
continuum

A ← Events capable of inducing absence → B

Attendance
and absence
behaviour

| Frequency of absence | Frequency of attendance |

Source: Nigel Nicholson (1977), 'Absence Behavior and Attendance Motivation: A Conceptual Synthesis',
Journal of Management Studies, *14*(13). p. 251.
Copyright © Basil Blackwell Ltd.

orientations or attitudes to work differ according to occupational experience and background, reflected, for example, in higher levels of absence among manual than among non-manual workers. Thirdly, the nature of jobs and the opportunities they provide for satisfaction and involvement vary, as again reflected in the differences between manual and non-manual worker absence. A fourth influence arises out of the rules of the workplace, which may be either strict or lenient on absence. A final influence is referred to as 'random' and refers to domestic or travel difficulties which may affect the ability to attend.

The result is an absence continuum, ranging from unavoidable influences (A), which impact on frequency of absence, to avoidable influences (B), which impact on frequency of attendance. Nicholson argues that absence-control policies should be aimed at tackling the avoidable influences, recognising that these will vary between individuals and work settings. For example, a minor ailment experienced by an older worker performing heavy manual work may be more likely to result in an absence than the same ailment experienced by a younger worker performing light office work, and if an organisation seeks to set targets for achievement, these differences must be recognised. The model provides a useful focus on a range of factors that influence attendance and non-attendance and that absence-management policies have to address, with an emphasis on those absences which may be seen as 'avoidable' in a specific organisational context. These will be explored in more detail later in the chapter.

Steers and Rhodes' (1978) 'process model of employee attendance' (Figure 2) starts from the characteristics of the job, which in turn influence job satisfaction and motivation to attend. Like Nicholson, these authors recognise that job satisfaction and motivation are in turn affected by personal characteristics which influence attendance – for example, that older age affects the likelihood of sickness, and that higher-educational attainments are more likely to lead to the pursuit of a career or profession with which lower absence levels are associated.

The model also incorporates the idea of 'pressures to attend'. In times of economic uncertainty, for example, fear

Figure 2 RHODES AND STEERS' MODEL OF EMPLOYEE ATTENDANCE

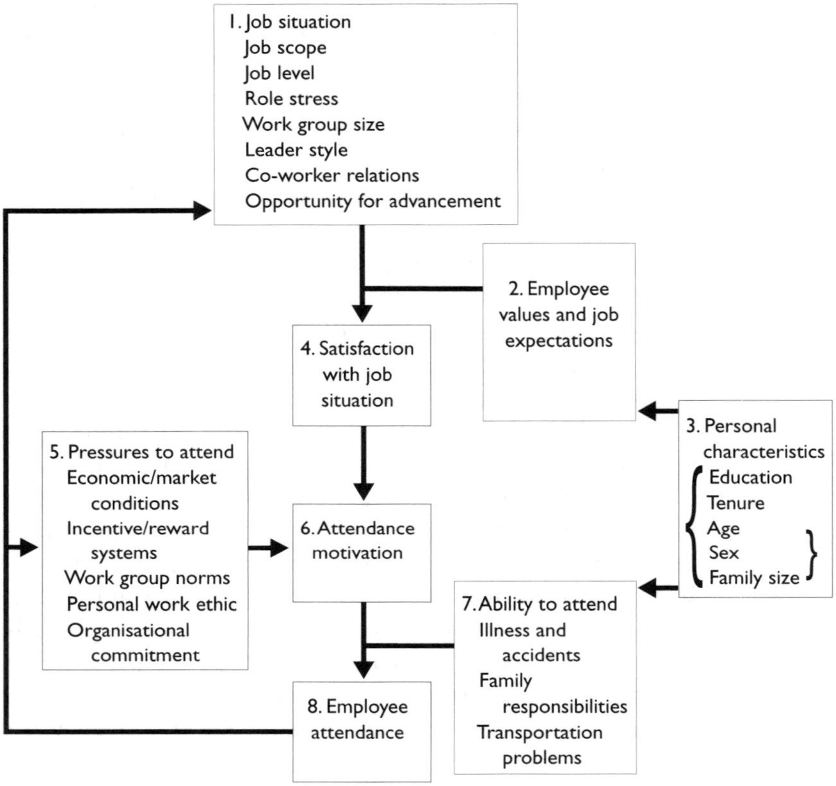

1. Job situation
   Job scope
   Job level
   Role stress
   Work group size
   Leader style
   Co-worker relations
   Opportunity for advancement

2. Employee values and job expectations

3. Personal characteristics
   Education
   Tenure
   Age
   Sex
   Family size

4. Satisfaction with job situation

5. Pressures to attend
   Economic/market conditions
   Incentive/reward systems
   Work group norms
   Personal work ethic
   Organisational commitment

6. Attendance motivation

7. Ability to attend
   Illness and accidents
   Family responsibilities
   Transportation problems

8. Employee attendance

Source: Rhodes and Steers, 1990. p. 46, © Addison-Wesley

of losing one's job may result in pressures not to be absent. Work-group or peer pressures may act either to encourage absence or attendance, according to the prevailing cultural norms. Loss of pay or an attendance bonus may also act to discourage absence. Finally, like Nicholson's, the model recognises the role of ability to attend. Circumstances arise, even for the most highly motivated employee, in which attendance is not possible. Genuine illness is one obvious example, as are family responsibilities and travel difficulties. Ability to attend is also influenced by the employee's personal circumstances. For example, size of family is likely to increase constraints on ability to attend, as is distance from home to work or the complexity of the journey undertaken. Absence patterns thus vary between individuals according to the particular influences on their behaviour. From a management perspective, the model therefore stresses the importance of understanding the prevailing influences on absence for each group of employees and applying the appropriate policies.

Subsequently, Rhodes and Steers (1990) developed what they term a 'diagnostic model of employee attendance' for use by managers in understanding absence in their organisations. This is illustrated in Figure 3, which recognises three key influences on attendance motivation.

First, organisational practices must set out clear attendance

Figure 3 **A DIAGNOSTIC MODEL OF EMPLOYEE ATTENDANCE**

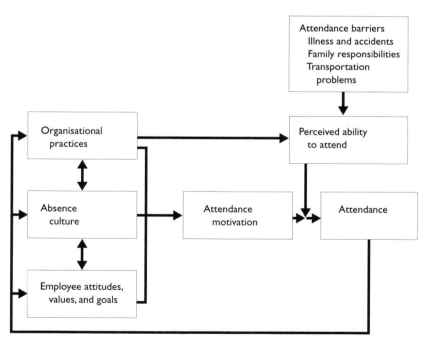

Source: Rhodes and Steers, 1990. p. 57, © Addison-Wesley

standards and procedures, pay due attention to work design, involve recruitment and selection practices that screen for past absence behaviour, and incorporate the communication of clear attendance standards to staff. Second, the importance of absence cultures should be recognised. In the absence of appropriate control policies, employee behaviours are likely to reflect the norms of the work group, which may either stress attendance or encourage absence. In addition to clear attendance standards, absence cultures can be influenced by attention to work design and the establishment of self-managing teams with highly interdependent roles. The third area of influence is on employee attitudes, values and goals which are in turn strongly influenced by the kinds of organisational practices and cultures considered above.

The diagnostic model also incorporates factors which may act as barriers to attendance – such as illness, family responsibilities and travel problems – but which may also be influenced by organisational policies. Although organisations are unlikely to want genuinely sick employees to come to work, company healthcare programmes, occupational health services and employee-assistance programmes can all help to create a healthier workforce. Various approaches are available to reduce absence arising out of family responsibilities – for example, childcare facilities, special leave or flexibility to allow occasional working from home. Travel difficulties may be alleviated through the provision of company bus services, car pooling or other arrangements.

Now that we have considered a number of models, the remainder of the chapter will examine in more detail the various factors included in these models and assess their significance as potential causes of absence. The various factors will be scrutinised under three headings: first, differences in absence due to the personal characteristics of individuals; second, factors within the direct influence of organisations; and third, factors external to the workplace.

The influence of personal characteristics on absence

The personal characteristics identified by Rhodes and Steers (1990) and Huczynski and Fitzpatrick (1989) are:

- length of service
- age
- gender
- personality
- employee attitudes, values and expectations
- past absence behaviour.

Length of service

It might be expected that absence would decrease with length of service as employees form ties of loyalty with the organisation and, where internal labour market hierarchies operate, they achieve promotion to higher grade or status positions by virtue of service. The research findings provide some support for a link between longer service and lower absence, but in practice the linkage is complicated by other factors that can also affect absence levels (Huczynski and Fitzpatrick, 1989). For example, many organisations provide occupational sick pay only after certain periods of service, and some increase entitlement with service. As we have noted and will return to again, there is evidence linking the payment of sick pay with higher absence levels, since the costs of absence to the individual become less where sick pay is provided. Absence levels could rise with service for this reason. Also, length of service is associated with age, which in turn has characteristic influences on absence, as we shall see shortly. In conclusion, then, length of service may be one factor that influences absence levels, but it is not a decisive one.

Age

There is general agreement from the research that younger people tend to have more frequent short spells of absence whereas older people have fewer short spells but are absent longer in each spell, especially after the age of 50, (Huczynski and Fitzpatrick, 1989). In terms of time lost by age, Barnby *et al*'s (1999) analysis of the data generated by the government's General Household Surveys and Labour Force Surveys between 1971 and 1997 reveals patterns of absence by age. Men's absence is constant at a little over 2 per cent of time lost up to age 40 and increases thereafter, peaking at about

7.5 per cent for 60- to 64-year-olds. Women's absence rises from around 3 per cent to about 4 per cent from entry into the job market as school-leavers to their early thirties, stabilises at this level until their early forties, then rises steadily to peak at 7 per cent at age 60. After normal retirement age, the absence rate falls for both genders, which the authors suggest is due to a 'sorting effect' as only those employees in better health tend to remain in work. Age is, therefore, an important factor in absence, especially in the pattern of absence that consists of frequent short spells which is often seen as more disruptive.

Gender

The general pattern which emerges from statistics on absence is that females have higher rates than males, although this pattern is inconsistent. Barnby *et al*'s (1997) data for the period from 1971 to 1997, referred to in the section above, shows that male and female absences were approximately the same during the 1970s, but from the early to mid-1980s onwards the female rate rose while the male rate fell over the remainder of the period to 1997. It seems likely that the increase in female absence during this period reflects the growing proportion of females with young children or other caring responsibilities in the labour force, a point to which we shall return below. In terms of recent statistical evidence, the major annual absence surveys by the CBI and CIPD do not report on absence by gender, although the issue has been explored in occasional surveys by IRS (1998) and the Industrial Society (1997, 2001). IRS (1998) found that only a quarter of their 182 respondents were able to report on absence statistics by gender, and within this small sample male absence stood at 2.5 per cent and female at 3.4 per cent. The Industrial Society's surveys analysed absence by gender but have reported contrary findings. In 1997, male absence stood at 2.5 per cent and female absence at 3.1 per cent; in 2001, male absence was 2.6 per cent, but female absence 2.2 per cent.

As with length of service discussed above, the underlying explanation for this apparently higher female absence rate may not lie in the gender difference *per se* but rather in other variables that affect male and female roles, both at work and in the wider society. By way of example, there is evidence that female absence falls as the age of dependent children rises (Huczynski and Fitzpatrick, 1989), indicating that some female absence results from a woman's role as carer in the family, involving the consequent need to take time off to look after sick children or elderly relatives. The role of family responsibilities has been recognised as a constraint on the ability of individuals to attend work in various studies of the causes of absence, and will be reviewed again in a later section on external influences. In addition, explanations of female absence patterns can also be found that relate to occupational structures, since a higher proportion of females than males occupies lower occupational positions, and a lower proportion reaches senior roles with which lower absence rates may be associated as a result of different career values and expectations. There is no evidence, for example, that women occupying senior positions have absence levels any higher than those of men in equivalent roles (Huczynski and Fitzpatrick, 1989). This raises some questions. In that family responsibilities may be a cause of female absence, the answer may lie in the ability of women in higher-paid roles to afford domestic assistance. Clearly, influence of gender on absence is complex, and gender of itself may be a less important explanation for absence than other independent variables which affect women's work and women's roles in the wider society.

Personality

Absence research has indicated that a relatively high proportion of absence within any particular workforce can be attributed to a relatively small proportion of the total workforce. This is, of course, a well-known phenomenon sometimes known as the '80/20 rule' and is attributed to the Italian economist Vilfredo Pareto. In the case of absence, it has been found, for example, that up to half of all absence can be accounted for by as little as 5 to 10 per cent of the workforce (Huczynski and Fitzpatrick, 1989). Absence research has endeavoured to investigate this phenomenon by attempting to identify personality factors that might lead an individual to become 'absence-prone'. Over the last decade or so, general agreement has emerged that there are five important personality traits (known as the 'big 5') which are valid predictors of job performance. These are: introversion/ extraversion, emotional stability, agreeableness, conscientiousness, and openness to experience (Roberts, 1997). The measurement of these traits lies at the heart of occupational testing, and one factor – conscientiousness – has been found to be a particularly effective predictor of job performance (Roberts, 1997). In relation to the links between the 'big 5' personality factors and absence, research by Judge *et al* (1997) found that two were moderately strong predictors. Extraversion was related to higher absence rates, and conscientiousness to lower absence rates.

Stress is also a factor in absence, and people's abilities to cope with it vary according to personality characteristics – a key one being what is known as the 'locus of control'. This personality attribute sees people as broadly divided into two personality types: 'internals' who perceive themselves as having a high degree of control over factors influencing their lives, and 'externals' who see themselves as the pawns of fate, their lives largely directed by external forces over which they have little or no control. Research has shown that 'internals' feel better able to take control of and directly influence stressful situations, in comparison with 'externals' who are more likely to experience greater stress because of their feeling of inability to control it. 'Externals' are also more likely to experience poorer health and higher absence rates than 'internals' (Robbins, 1993). It may be concluded that personality differences do influence absence levels – but interesting though all this is, for all practical purposes there is not much that organisations can do about it!

Employee attitudes, values and expectations

This is a complex issue that has attracted a good deal of attention on the part of industrial sociologists and psychologists over many years, and anything approaching a full discussion is beyond the scope of the present text. In any event, there is no general agreement and the issue is one of considerable debate. Clearly, attitudes, values and expectations will depend partly on factors outside the workplace as a result of family, education, community, class and other influences in people's upbringings. They will also be influenced by the experience of work generally, and for some people activities other than work will be more central to their life goals. Where family responsibilities, hobbies or other non-work interests take precedence, it might reasonably be expected that this will be conducive to higher absence (Rhodes and Steers, 1990). At the same time, attitudes can change – for example, as a result of experience in an organisational setting. For our purposes we can assume that absence behaviour will in part result from attitudes, values and behaviour personal to individuals, formed outside the workplace, but also recognise that attitudes may either change or be reinforced by the prevailing culture of the organisation and the controls operated by management. This is a topic to which we shall return in this chapter and elsewhere in this book.

Past absence behaviour

Research indicates that one of the strongest indicators of future absence behaviour is past absence behaviour – and, moreover, that absence frequency has been found to be a stronger predictor than total number of days lost (Rhodes and Steers, 1990; Huczynski and Fitzpatrick, 1989). Whatever the reasons, this finding has clear implications for the screening process at recruitment – and this is a matter to which we shall return in the next chapter.

The influence of the organisational context

The influence of the organisational context as a cause of absence may be seen from four distinct perspectives:

☐ work design
☐ other job-related factors
☐ work group norms and cultures
☐ organisational policies and practices in relation to absence.

The components of each of these perspectives will be examined in turn in this section.

Work design

There has for many years been considerable discussion about the impact of the design of jobs on employee attitudes and behaviours, in terms of motivation, commitment, quality of work and so on, and some of this discussion has extended to absenteeism. The 'scientific management' approach to the design of work tended to predominate in the twentieth century and is based on the principles of a high degree of division of labour and specialisation, with the general result that many work roles consist mainly of simple, fragmented, routine and repetitive tasks. Such ideas are popularly associated with the 'scientific management' approach advocated by the American engineer F. W. Taylor (1911) and also reflect the predominant influence of people with engineering training in the design of jobs in modern organisations. The stereotyped image is of the production-line worker, but there is a view that the division of labour, task specialisation and deskilling have gone far beyond this to affect most jobs in some way (Braverman, 1974). Offices are thus seen as 'white-collar factories', and even management jobs have become functionally specialised to the extent that one department has little idea of what goes on in another. The advantages of such an approach are usually expressed in terms of the efficiency gains of specialisation. By implication, each individual is capable only of assimilating and deploying a limited range of expertise in a specific field, and by focusing on this field alone he or she becomes proficient. The disadvantages of such an approach have long been recognised. Where it has been carried to extremes, the results have been boredom, apathy and minimal commitment to the job and organisation. More recently, some wider ramifications have also been recognised. Task specialisation, leading to a narrow and inflexible skills base within the workforce, has done little to equip people to adapt to rapid changes in the environment, with the result that they are likely to resist changes that threaten the narrow skills base from which they draw their livelihood. Moreover, it has done little to encourage learning as the starting-point for adapting to rapid change. Given also the recognition of quality as a key factor in competitiveness, traditional work fragmentation has tended to diffuse responsibility for quality, the effects of which were plain to see until the recent growth of interest in this topic.

It is now pertinent to enquire into the potential effects of traditional approaches to work design on absence. Common sense would suggest that employees who experience routine and repetitive work, with low levels of autonomy, responsibility and decision-making, are likely to experience minimal commitment to their jobs and may be more likely to take time off. Rhodes and Steers (1990) conclude from their review of the research into the general effects of scientific management on job design that 'negative outcomes include lower job satisfaction, lower motivation and higher absenteeism'. They go on to argue, on the basis of a review of absence studies carried in the mid- to late 1980s, that investigations into 'the relationship between job satisfaction dimensions and absenteeism have uniformly found that the strongest relationship exists between work satisfaction and [low] absence frequency'. They conclude that lack of job involvement is particularly closely concerned with absence frequency. In a similar vein, Huczynski and Fitzpatrick (1989) conclude that 'a great deal of research associates high levels of task repetitiveness with low job satisfaction [which] in turn has been positively correlated with absence'. Surveys of managers' opinions about the causes of absence also tend to bear this out. Nearly two thirds of respondents to the Industrial Society's (2001) absence survey felt that motivating staff was the most effective way of managing absence, placing this top of a list of a dozen or so possible absence-control measures. The consensus of opinion thus appears to be that routine, repetitive and fragmented tasks under traditional scientific management approaches to job design are likely to lead to higher absence frequency. If this is so, it should be expected that initiatives to redesign jobs to reduce their routine, repetitive and fragmented nature ought to have the opposite effect – of lowering absence frequency – and this is a question to which we shall return in Chapter 4.

Other job-related factors

In addition to the important issue of job design, a number of other job-related factors have been identified by Huczynski and Fitzpatrick (1989) as having an influence on absence, and they are briefly reviewed in this section.

Stress

Against a background of downsizing and de-layering and increased pressures on individuals to deliver high perform-ance, it is now recognised that work-related stress can affect all levels in the organisational hierarchy. Carroll (1996) quotes research sources that indicate that typically 20 per cent of a given workforce suffers from mental illness and 30 to 40 per cent of all sickness absence involves mental illness or emotional stress.

Cary Cooper (in Huczynski and Fitzpatrick, 1989) identified a number of causes of stress at work. The first relates to the conditions in which a job is performed. Poor working con-ditions, physical dangers, even the distractions created in an open-plan office all cause stress. Research has shown that factories that have poor standards of housekeeping or poorly equipped or maintained machinery, or offices which are drably furnished, poorly lit or poorly heated, can have higher absence levels.

A second cause of stress is shiftwork, although its relation-ship to absence is not entirely clear. Warr and Yearta (1995) found that shiftworkers were more likely than others to be absent for sickness or injury. This was particularly marked among male shiftworkers on two-shift schedules or rotating three-shift cycles, but less so among females.

A third cause of stress has to do with work overload or underload (including repetitive work or periods of low activity, causing boredom between periods of high activity). Studies have connected both work overload and underload with absence. Bevan and Hayday (1998) noted a relationship between the prolonged working of excessive hours and absence among staff below management level.

A fourth cause has to do with role ambiguity (lack of clarity about what is expected) and role conflict (where the expectations are clear, but they conflict with each other). Role conflict can also arise where there is conflict between work demands and other non-work roles, such as the family. Research has shown that role ambiguity and role conflict are both causes of stress, higher absence and serious illness.

A fifth factor relates to career development. There are two aspects here: overpromotion, associated with difficulties in coping, and underpromotion, associated with feelings of lack of status or recognition and stifled career ambitions. Bevan and Hayday (1998) argued that career dissatisfaction is one of the most powerful predictors of absence, as well as being linked to the likelihood of leaving.

Other factors include poor relationships at work, lack of consultation and little participation in decision-making. Stress is increasingly being recognised as a significant cause of workplace absence and, in the opinion of respondents to both the Gee (1999) and CIPD (2000) surveys on absence, was the second most important cause of time lost. The issues raised in this section are wide-reaching, encompassing working conditions, patterns of working hours, workloads, career and promotional prospects and workplace relationships, not to mention stress caused by factors outside the workplace, and serve to indicate just how broad and comprehensive absence-control programmes may have to be.

Frequency of job moves

As has long been recognised, work fulfils social needs for many people, involving opportunities to form ties of loyalty with work colleagues. There is some evidence that where employees are required to move frequently within their workplaces to meet the needs of flexibility or where systems of job rotation are in place, the negative effect of this on people's social needs can result in higher absence.

Leadership style

A number of studies have identified links between the style of first-line supervisors and absence behaviour in work groups. For example, employees who feel more able to discuss their problems with their supervisor have been found to go absent less than those who felt unable to do so.

Organisation and work group size

National surveys of absence have consistently shown that total days lost through absence rise fairly consistently with the total number of people employed. So, for example, the CBI (2000) found absence rates of around 2 per cent in organisations of less than 50 employees, rising to just over 3 per cent for organisations employing 50 to 500, and reaching around 4 per cent in organisations employing more than 500 people. The reasons for this are not entirely clear but are likely to be bound up with the process of bureaucratisation and the tendency for work group sizes to become larger and for work roles to become more specialised in bigger organisations. In smaller organisations individuals' roles are likely to be more visible and multiskilled and less easily covered during absence, making the impact of their absence more disruptive and more noticeable to colleagues and management. Such visibility becomes less in larger organisations, which may have more scope to provide cover and where absences become less noticeable within the multiple layers of supervision and management. Recent moves towards de-layering, decentralisation to strategic business units, empowerment and multitasking within larger enterprises may have the effect of reducing the influence of organisation size on absence behaviour, but this has yet to be substantiated by research evidence.

Work group norms and cultures

The influence of work-group norms on behaviour has been recognised since the famous Hawthorne experiments of the 1920s and 1930s (Roethlisberger and Dickson, 1939). We noted earlier, in our consideration of the 'adjustment to work' models of absence behaviour, that absence levels may be associated with the process of both formal and informal organisational socialisation. The formal process of socialisation involves the communication of the organisation's rules and standards of conduct, reinforced (or not, as the case may be) by the subsequent behaviour of those authorised to enforce them. People fairly quickly get to understand whether the rules operate in practice or whether they are just part of management rhetoric and can effectively be ignored. Informal socialisation occurs where new employees, on arrival within their work group, fairly quickly learn what behaviour is appropriate. In the case of absence, they learn by observation the absence behaviours of the group and their consequences in terms of any action taken by superiors. Because most people want to be accepted by the group of which they are a part, they tend to conform to the established norms: groups will often bring a range of pressures to bear to ensure that behavioural norms are enforced. Norms can be of various types, but probably the most common relate to standards of performance, of which absence is a part. Norms arise, therefore, out of the formal rules established by management and the rigour with which management enforces them on the one hand, and the informal rules established by work groups on the other – the latter being strongly influenced by the former. Formal and informal norms are therefore closely interrelated.

A powerful source of norms is 'custom and practice' – an informal process of joint accommodation between managers, supervisors and work groups about what behaviour is accepted. Custom and practice has its roots in the history of management and work-group relationships in a given workplace; it sets precedents and establishes powerful expectations about what behaviours are acceptable and what disciplinary sanctions will be applied when acceptable norms of behaviour are transgressed. The 'rules' generated by custom and practice form precedents based on the past action taken by management in specific situations and are reinforced by notions of fairness and equity. Where certain transgressions (such as absence) have been overlooked in the past, there will be powerful expectations on the part of the work group that they will also be overlooked in the future on grounds of consistency and fairness. The opposite will also be true – there will be expectations within the work group that past penalties for specific offences will also be applied in the future. Custom and practice is the outcome of the relative bargaining power of management to enforce sanctions and the work group to resist them. This process may either be formal, reinforced by trade union action in support of their members in disciplinary situations, or informal, part of the daily process of accommodation and 'give-and-take' between supervisors and work groups in order to maintain morale and good will.

It will be evident from the foregoing discussion that not just the words but also the actions of managements have an important influence on establishing acceptable norms of behaviour. Where certain types of absence (such as the odd day off, or indeed absence in general) have tended to be overlooked in the past, there will strong expectations that they will continue to be so in the future. Changing this situation requires managements to broadcast clear and powerful signals that there is to be a break with the past.

So far, absence culture has been seen as part of a process of negotiated agreement between management and work groups in which the enforcement of rules plays a significant role in establishing norms and expectations. There can be little doubt that organisational policies and practices, whether established unilaterally by management or jointly agreed with trade unions, are important influences on absence – and we shall return to this theme in the next chapter. Another perspective on absence culture has also emerged more recently: the discipline of peer pressure associated with the idea of self-managing teams and its potential for absence reduction – and this is a theme to which we shall also be returning.

Organisational practices and policies

Organisational policies and practices regarding attendance and absence are conventionally viewed in the literature on absence management as part of the 'cure' for absenteeism, not its cause. In this respect, the present publication is no different, and a range of policies for absence reduction is examined in Chapter 3. However, it would also be sensible to look at current policies as part of the cause of absence, since cause and effect are closely interrelated. This section of the chapter has been concerned with the organisational context of absence. By implication, the causes of absence considered here result from decisions consciously or unconsciously made by managements, and therefore lie within their power to alter. So if the research suggests that traditional, fragmented job roles involving routine and repetitive tasks, the minimum of variety and a lack opportunities to learn new skills tend to encourage higher absence levels, it is open to managements to think up alternative ways of organising tasks to be undertaken by flexible, self-managing teams which the research suggests tend to encourage higher attendance levels. If lack of any clear framework of rules, or the consistent application of any framework of rules established, has encouraged cultural norms that tolerate certain levels of absence, the responsibility for changing this position lies entirely within the remit of an organisation's management.

It is not necessary here to extend this discussion further, for a more comprehensive review of the options available for absence control makes up much of the next chapter, but suffice to note that causes and consequences are closely interrelated.

It is worth concluding this section by focusing on one aspect of organisational policies that has received some attention in the research – the links between an organisation's sick pay policies and levels of absence. The general conclusion from Britain and other countries is that where more generous sickness benefits are provided, absence levels tend to rise. This has been found to be so either where the costs of sickness benefit are met mainly by the state (as in Germany) or where they are met through employers' occupational sick pay schemes, as in Britain or the United States (Huczynksi and Fitzpatrick, 1989). Research has also shown that employees in organisations not covered by occupational sick pay – such as those with short service or on temporary contracts – have lower levels of absence than employees who are covered by such schemes (Huczynski and Fitzpatrick, 1989). A related issue is the emergence of cultural expectations to the effect that a certain amount of paid sick leave is an 'entitlement' to be taken, rather like paid holiday entitlement. This possibility was considered by the respondents to the CBI's (2001) absence survey to be the second most significant cause of manual worker absence after 'general sickness'. It is not being suggested here that organisations should do away with sick pay because it encourages absence, but rather that the management of absence should be subject to closer control so that potential abuses are minimised. This is a topic to which we shall also return.

The influence of external factors on absence

In this section of the chapter we consider a range of potential causes of absence that emanate mainly from outside the workplace and may therefore lie outside the immediate control of managements – although there are certain initiatives available to help control even these external influences. The main external influences on absence, which were viewed by the models considered at the beginning of the chapter as restricting employees' 'ability to attend', are:

☐ economic and market conditions

☐ genuine illness and accidents

☐ travel and transport problems

☐ family responsibilities.

Each of these is considered in turn below.

Economic and market conditions

Research provides some evidence that employees' propensity to attend or take time off is related to their perceptions of the state of the job market. During times of economic boom, relatively lower levels of unemployment and plentiful job vacancies, people feel more secure in their jobs or more confident of their ability to find another one, and are more prepared to take time off. Conversely, in times of recession, higher unemployment and less job security, the reverse is true and absence levels tend to fall. Such behaviour may be more conspicuous where absence levels form one of the criteria used for redundancy selection which, according to IRS (1995b, 1998), has increasingly become the case amongst employers in Britain – around a fifth applying this criterion. Partial support for the proposition that absence levels are affected by economic and market conditions can be found in the periodic national surveys of absence conducted by the leading management or employer organisations. The CBI, for example, found that national absence rates rose amid the economic boom of the later 1980s but fell quite sharply in the recessionary conditions after 1991. Absence rates amongst all employees rose from 3.6 to 4 per cent between 1987 and 1991, fell back a little to around 3.5 per cent from 1992 to 1994, thereafter rising slightly with recovery to a peak in 1998, and falling again thereafter (CBI, 1993, 1997, 2001).

However, if this hypothesis were to be fully consistent it might be expected that regions of the country experiencing higher levels of unemployment might generally experience lower levels of absence – but the data from surveys such as that of the CBI do not confirm this. In its 2001 survey, for example, the region with the highest absence rate for manual workers (Northern Ireland) was also the region with the highest level of unemployment, while Greater London had the highest rate of manual worker absence but much lower levels of unemployment. Differences may in part be explained by variations in the occupational structure of a specific region, particularly where male manuals (who tend to have higher levels of absence) make up a larger proportion of total employment in the region.

We may conclude, therefore, that organisations experience rises and falls in overall absence levels according to changes in economic and market conditions, but such fluctuations do not appear to be particularly significant. As outlined in the Introduction to this book, much more significant are the differences in absence level between organisations in the same industry – differences which remain constant whatever the economic or market conditions in that industry. The actions pursued by management within an organisation seem to be more influential on absence levels than the impact of economic or market factors.

Genuine illness and accidents

The existence of genuine illness as a cause of absence seems obvious, yet it is sometimes neglected in writings on the subject which tend to imply that the problem of absenteeism can be solved totally through the application of the appropriate policies. Although it is impossible to be certain about the extent to which genuine illness features in total absence statistics, 70 per cent of respondents to the CIPD's (2000) absence survey considered that genuine illness was the major contributor to time lost among manual workers, and 80 per cent thought this to be so in the case of non-manual workers. It has been estimated that genuine illness accounts for between a half and two thirds of all absence (Huczynski and Fitzpatrick, 1989), and this is borne out by the respondents to the CIPD's (2001) absence survey who estimated that two thirds of absence was the result of ill-health, whereas a third of absence recorded as sickness was not perceived to be health-related. Research has shown that sickness absence, especially among males, is age-related, an increase in absence levels occurring after the age of 40 and increasing more sharply after the age of 50 (Warr and Yearta, 1995).

We also noted earlier the potential contribution of stress, both work- and non-work-related, and it is estimated that this may account for up to 40 per cent of all sickness absence. The significance of stress has also featured in surveys of managers' opinions about the causes of absence. In the CIPD's (2001) survey, stress was rated as an important cause of absence among non-manual workers, mentioned by 42 per cent of respondents and seen as the second most important cause of absence after minor illnesses such as colds/flu, stomach upsets and headaches.

A further factor is alcohol-related absence which the DSS has estimated to account for 5 per cent of days lost through sickness absence per annum.

In all, therefore, genuine sickness absence must be seen as a major cause of days lost, but one which more and more organisations are seeking to tackle through the rapid rise in employee assistance programmes, counselling and other initiatives to promote better health awareness.

Travel and transport problems

A number of studies have shown that transport and travel difficulties can affect people's ability to attend work even if they are motivated to do so. Associated factors include the length of the journey to work, weather conditions, traffic congestion, and the standard of public transport services. Studies have tended to show that the longer the journey – especially if exacerbated by bad weather or traffic congestion – the greater the likelihood that people will give up or not even attempt it. Although these factors may be seen as largely outside the control of employers, they could be taken into account when making recruitment and selection decisions, when making decisions about the location of workplaces, or when contemplating the provision of transport services for employees where the final part of the journey to a workplace is subject to poor public-service provision.

Family responsibilities

We noted earlier that one factor which contributes to gender differences in absence statistics relates to responsibilities for the family – dependent children and elderly relatives may affect the ability of women to attend work – and, no doubt, a proportion of male absence can be attributed to this factor also. Research has shown that up to 15 per cent of all people at work are carers, rising to a quarter in the 45 to 64 age-group (Evans, 1998). Research also indicates that women's absence rates increase with family size, but decline as the age of dependent children increases. The overall absence statistics for women show that absence rates also decline as they get older (Huczynski and Fitzpatrick, 1989). This provides fairly strong evidence in support of the view that family responsibilities are a significant cause of absence. Moreover, that view is supported by the opinions expressed by managers in absence surveys. In the Industrial Society's (1997) survey, more than half of the managers identified sickness in the family, childcare problems and other domestic responsibilities as significant causes of absence, placing it third in a league table of causes after colds and flu and stress/personal problems. A similar view was taken by the managers responding to the CBI's (1997) absence survey, nearly half of them rating family responsibilities as a major cause of absence, second only to genuine illness. More recent surveys suggest – at least in the perception of respondents – that home and family responsibilities have become less significant causes of absence (CBI, 2001), and just a quarter of respondents to the CIPD's (2000) absence survey saw them as a significant cause of absence among manual workers. The reasons for this are open to speculation but may reflect the statutory provisions introduced in 1999 for reasonable time off to deal with domestic problems relating to children or close relatives, and may also reflect an increase in employers' voluntary policies of enhancing dependant leave beyond the statutory provisions (Evans, 2001). Family responsibilities should, nevertheless, be seen as a potentially significant cause of absence and can inspire employees otherwise properly motivated to respond by placing family needs over pressures to attend work. This highlights the need to ensure that policies to reduce absence are appropriate to the cause. For example, family responsibilities are an aspect of absence which employers may seek to influence through flexible working time arrangements, creches or other special leave arrangements.

Conclusions

As is evident from the information presented in this chapter, absence is a complex topic and its causes are many and varied. We have considered these causes under three broad headings: personal characteristics, organisational policies, and external factors which act to inhibit individuals' abilities to attend. Although some of these influences may be outside the control of employers, it is possible to identify a host of causes of absence which can be tackled through the implementation of the appropriate policies. These causes in summary are:

☐ employee attitudes and expectations
☐ lack of appropriate organisational controls
☐ rigid and inflexible job design and lack of empowerment
☐ lack of opportunities for teamworking
☐ poor working conditions and environment
☐ work overload or underload
☐ frustrated career and promotion prospects

☐ interpersonal problems in the workplace

☐ ineffective screening at recruitment and selection

☐ stress, caused either within the workplace or outside it

☐ inappropriate management styles

☐ an organisational culture that fails to discourage absence

☐ lack of priority given to the promotion of workforce health and wellbeing

☐ failure to recognise the significance of domestic responsibilities and a lack of flexibility in employment policies.

The implementation of policies to tackle these issues is the subject of the next chapter.

3 ABSENCE CONTROL AND ATTENDANCE-MANAGEMENT POLICIES

In Chapter 1 we looked at measuring, costing, monitoring and benchmarking absence, and in Chapter 2 we considered the causes of absence. This chapter outlines the policy options that employers have for *controlling* absence. Because 'controlling absence' sounds negative – and evidence suggests that policies aimed purely at control can actually lead to higher absence by undermining employee commitment – managers nowadays increasingly look to *manage* absence – that is, to create an environment in which employees are more likely to want to come to work than to stay at home. As we shall see, survey analysis suggests that this latter approach tends to be the most successful in reducing absence levels. With its emphasis on incentives, teamworking and employee involvement, managing absence approaches also seem closer to human resource philosophies than traditional personnel management attitudes.

What sort of policies?

The main objective of absence policies is really to encourage people to want to come to work when they would rather be at home (although no good employer sets out to pressurise the genuinely ill to return to work before they are well enough to do so). Incidences of absence therefore fall on a continuum running from genuine ill-health at one extreme, which demands one set of policies, to lack of motivation at the other, which requires totally different approaches. In between are any number of combinations of ill-health and motivation which policies must tackle.

Because it is a complex subject, there is no universal panacea for managing absence. There are, however, a whole raft of policies employers can choose from. Between 15 and 18 approaches are listed by Bevan and Hayday (1998), the CBI (2001) and the CIPD (2001), but others (eg Scott and Markham, 1982) have found up to 34 different policies. Not all of them were necessarily originally introduced to reduce absence, but that does seem to have been one by-product of their adoption.

It is now generally recognised that a two-pronged approach to absence and attendance management is required which contains both of the following elements:

- □ policies to manage and discourage absence
- □ policies which positively encourage attendance.

This chapter explores each of these two kinds of policies in turn.

Policies to manage and discourage absence

The main policies for managing absence are :

- □ absence strategies, policies and targets
- □ enhancing the role of the line manager
- □ involving employees and trade unions
- □ absence monitoring
- □ return-to-work interviews
- □ establishing trigger-points
- □ absence review and counselling meetings
- □ disciplinary procedures
- □ using absence as a criterion for redundancy selection.

Absence strategies, policies and targets

Before we look at policies in more detail, it is important to emphasise that the foundation of an effective absence management strategy is to have a written absence management policy, with full and visible top management commitment. According to the CIPD's (2001) absence survey, 80 per cent of respondents had a written absence management policy, a figure which rose to over 90 per cent amongst organisations employing 2,000 or more. MacDonald (2001) provides the following example policy statement:

> The Company aims to encourage all its employees to maximise their attendance at work . . . Where an employee is genuinely sick and unable to attend work, it is the Company's policy to continue salary for certain defined periods of time and to offer security of employment during such periods. A procedure is in place which explains fully employees' obligations towards the employer in the event of sickness absence. This covers the employee's duty to notify the Company in the event that he or she is unable to attend work due to sickness, the requirements to produce self-certificates and doctors' certificates, the employer's right to ask for a medical report, return-to-work interviews, and employees' entitlements to statutory and contractual sick pay.

In addition to the policy statement, there must be clear absence procedures set out in more detail in employee handbooks. Policies and procedures must strike a fair balance between the sanctions available to the employer and the steps that he or she will take to encourage attendance and assist those who have a genuine health problem.

It also appears that organisations are increasingly setting targets for achievement in relation to time lost through absence. Both IRS (1998) and Gee (1999) found that around a third of organisations set targets, typically to bring absence down to between 2 and 4 per cent of time lost. The CIPD (2001) found that 42 per cent of organisations had targets to limit absence to around 3 per cent of time lost, perhaps indicative of a growing interest in target-setting and a tightening of the targets set compared with the survey findings of three or four years previously. The CIPD also found that of those organisations with targets, 84 per cent thought that their targeted reductions were achievable.

Enhancing the role of the line manager

In the line manager two important threads of successful absence management come together: the measurement and monitoring of absence figures, and the implementation of absence policies. A feature of devolved organisations is the empowering of line managers to manage their staff, within guidelines prepared by the personnel department, but with a very hands-off personnel approach – at least until a stage where the disciplinary procedure is invoked. Our case studies, and others reported elsewhere, emphasise the central role played by line managers in absence control.

At the most basic level, line managers are increasingly the major players in the collection of absence statistics – which makes sense because they are usually the first contact-point for employees who report sick. They are also the interface between management and managed, the people charged with implementing policies at the lowest level. The case studies at the end of this book – James Cropper plc and the Scottish Prison Service – both emphasise the importance of devolving responsibility for absence management to the line.

The common themes, therefore, are: first, disseminating absence information back to line managers as frequently as possible (monthly seems most favoured) and in as disaggregated a form as necessary. Computerised systems have a valuable role in enabling managers to be informed the instant an employee crosses a 'trigger-point' into a different phase of the absence policy. Second, absence targets are set, often centrally. Achievement against target is publicised so that performance is clear to all employees – some organisations go as far as to publish absence league tables to generate an element of competition between managers.

Line managers also need encouragement and guidance. Organisations do find that line managers can prefer to let absence policies wither through lack of use, particularly if they think – as they often seem to – that 'if you're sick, you're sick', and that is the end of the story, or that the policy is being less rigorously applied in some areas than others and that *senior managers are not themselves particularly committed to absence control.*

Assistance also comes from preparing written guidance and providing training so that managers know what is expected of them. That sounds self-evident, but IRS (1998) found that only 40 per cent of organisations in their survey trained line managers in handling absence. Both the recent absence surveys from the CIPD (2000, 2001) found similarly modest levels of manager training in relation to absence management. Yet according to the respondents to the Industrial Society's (2001) survey of attendance management practices, training managers in handling absences was rated the fourth most effective approach after motivating staff, return-to-work interviews and accurate monitoring.

A review by Evans (1999) of the typical content of employers' absence management training programmes found that they normally lasted for one or two days and contained information and guidance on the following elements:

- company absence policies and procedures
- the causes of absence
- the role of the manager/supervisor in absence management
- the legal and disciplinary aspects of short- and long-term absence
- the role of the company's occupational health service in absence management
- the operation (where applicable) of 'trigger-points'
- the development of skills in conducting return-to-work interviews
- the development of counselling skills and the techniques of problem-solving interviews
- the use of attendance- or absence-management software.

A key feature of any management training is the development of skills using exercises, videos and role plays; more information is given in Appendix 2 about the suppliers of materials for absence-management training and details of the types of materials available, including videos.

Involving line managers in absence control requires a big investment in training. It is not a one-off investment. Absence policies often develop over time to match changing circumstances, so keeping managers fully equipped to deal with the demands placed on them is a continuing process.

Involving employees and trade unions

Case-study evidence suggests that employers have actively tried to involve their employees and trade unions in designing and enforcing absence policies. IRS (1994) found that over a third of organisations provided their trade unions with absence statistics, and more recently LRD (1999) found that absence policies were discussed with the union at three quarters of the respondents' workplaces where they were recognised. The starting-point for attacking absence at Iveco Ford Trucks from the late 1980s to the mid-1990s, for example, was a sharing of information about absence with trade unions, leading to a new absence policy based around access to the sick-pay scheme, both agreed with the unions.

Employers say that unions often support management's attempts to control absence not least – as Iveco found – because they tend to get all the flak from members obliged to cover for absent colleagues. Usually the unions' primary objective is to ensure that policies are fair and equitable, not to condone unreasonable absence. The introduction of a computerised personnel system at European Components Corporation provided the ammunition which eventually forced the unions to acknowledge the scale of the absence problem at the company and to support management in its efforts to tackle it.

Some organisations have found that involving individual employees is also valuable. Attitude surveys can pinpoint the existence of an absence problem, help assess employees' own attitudes to absence, and identify approaches that might reduce it. There are plenty of anecdotal stories to suggest that employees dislike malingerers as much as employers: when managers choose to discipline those running taxi firms while on sick leave, or attending test matches in full view of the cameras, they are more likely to get employee support than not. But it is *management's* job to tackle absence, and it is unreasonable to expect employees to do it for them – if managers turn a blind eye to absence, so will employees. What managers can get through involving employees is their support for actions they see as fair and reasonable – and for policies to work, that seems essential.

Having said that, employers with 'carrot'-type incentives to reduce absence – especially where the benefit is earned in relation to group performance – find that employee peer-group pressure can be an important tool. Where all employees stand to lose a bonus, access to a generous sick pay scheme or free time, they do appear to exert a pressure on individuals to keep sick absence to a minimum. While this is a healthy attitude to foster, employers must be on their guard against peer-group pressure resulting in discrimination against groups perceived to be likely to have high absence rates (the chronically sick, or some people with disabilities), and against such pressure forcing the genuinely ill to come in to work.

Absence monitoring

We have said that line managers provide the interface with the bulk of employees and that organisations have increasingly devolved the day-to-day management of absence to them. A major feature of the line managers' role involves monitoring sick employees. This takes two forms: keeping in touch with people while they are off sick, and interviewing them on their return.

Keeping in touch with an employee need not be done in an overbearing way – reasonably regular phone-calls will do just to check how the employee is recovering and his or her likely date of return. It is important to talk to the employee direct, not to rely on talking to a member of the family (except in circumstances of hospitalisation, for example) or on reports from work colleagues along the lines of 'I saw old Joe on Saturday and he says he'll be off another three weeks.' Some companies (eg Nissan) carry out home visits. These can take two guises: first, where the employee is away on long-term sick leave and where visits have a distinct welfare element to them; and second, in cases where management have reason to believe an employee is abusing the system. Such visits can throw up interesting results. After fruitlessly knocking on the door of an absent employee, one line manager/personnel officer team was told by a neighbour that they were wasting their time because 'He always works on his market stall on Mondays.' That particular employee is no longer with the company, his case not helped by his claiming absence due to a bad back. Other cases include employees running taxi firms or working in pubs! But visits do have to be handled with care to ensure that to other employees they do not look like victimisation. Conversely, reactions can be somewhat negative. Shocked by a particularly high level of absence one Monday, the personnel officer of Northern Ireland company European Components Corporation carried out a number of home visits: the resulting industrial action led to a softening of that particular approach (Arkin, 1992).

According to Bevan and Hayday (1998), nearly half of the respondents to their survey had a policy which required managers to stay in touch during an employee's absence. The extent to which line managers get involved in home visits is less clear. Such evidence as there is presents a rather inconsistent picture. In a survey of over 300 employers by James *et al* (2002a, 2001b), around 40 per cent of respondents had a policy of maintaining contact and just under a third provided for home visits. By contrast, other surveys (eg Gee, 1999; CIPD, 2001) suggest that very few organisations use home visits, and IDS (1998) has indicated that where they are provided for they are more likely to be performed by occupational health staff.

Return-to-work interviews

The second major policy initiative carried out by line managers is the return-to-work interview. Absence surveys have consistently shown that return-to-work interviews are amongst the most widely-applied tools of absence management, in use by around two thirds of organisations (CBI, 2001; CIPD, 2001; IRS, 1998; Bevan and Hayday, 1998), although the CBI (2001) found their use in over three quarters of organisations in relation to non-manual staff absence. Gee (1999) found that the use of return-to-work interviews increased by organisation size, 90 per cent of larger organisations of over 2,000 people using them, 60 per cent of employers of 100 to 500 people doing so, whereas only a small proportion of employers of less than 100 used them automatically in every case. Assessments of the effectiveness of return-to-work interviews have also been generally positive, respondents to both the CBI (2001) and CIPD (2001) absence surveys rating them the most effective tool in absence management.

Return-to-work interviews are normally conducted by the employee's immediate supervisor or manager and serve a number of purposes in absence control. First, they are concerned to identify the cause of the absence and may also provide an opportunity to explore any particular problems which the employee may have. Second, they serve to indicate to employees that their absence was noticed and that they were missed. A failure to carry out such an interview may indicate to staff that absences do not matter or that what is said in absence policies is not actually applied in practice. This, in turn, may serve to create a culture in which employees perceive that absence will be tolerated. The third purpose of a return-to-work interview, then, is to demonstrate that absence is a high priority for the employer and that stated policies are also put into practice. Fourth, the return-to-work interview can usefully close by briefing the employee on anything that he or she might need to know which occurred during the absence. It is also important to emphasise that the return-to-work interview is not a disciplinary meeting, even though half the shopfloor respondents in an LRD survey (1999) said that in their view their employers used them in this way. At the same time, it is important that return-to-work interviews conclude by setting clear targets for improvement, make it clear that the achievement of these targets will be subject to monitoring and review, and make it clear to the employee the possible disciplinary consequences of failing to improve. It is important that return-to-work interviews are carried out by supervisors and managers after every instance of absence, without exception, and that they are carried out fairly and consistently. Supervisors and managers must be appropriately trained in how to conduct these interviews to help ensure that consistency is being achieved. Such training must focus on the techniques of 'problem-solving' interviews, and the use of counselling skills (see below) is likely to be appropriate. At Boots the Chemists

(Industrial Society, 1997), for example, managers are required to:

☐ enquire into the reason for the absence
☐ assess whether the reasons offered are consistent with other reliable available evidence
☐ raise any doubts with the member of staff
☐ allow the member of staff to explain the absence.

One of the difficulties experienced by organisations with policies of conducting return-to-work interviews is ensuring that they happen. Supervisors or managers experience many competing pressures on their time and it may be tempting to overlook the requirement to carry out the interview. One approach is to install some control mechanism which demands documentary evidence or a sign-off that the interview has taken place, such as a form to be returned to the personnel department. In any event it makes sense to keep some written record of the interview, which may become relevant if the formal disciplinary procedure has to be invoked at a future date.

Establishing trigger-points

Absence policies often consist of a number of stages starting with informal interviews and running through a gamut of formal warnings and referrals to occupational health practitioners to the ultimate sanction of dismissal. Guidance for managers usually sets out the sort of absence record which triggers each stage (although, of course, the disciplinary procedure can come in at any stage if there is real abuse). This is not always the case, however, and some organisations apply the absence policy on a case-by-case basis or take account of where an individual's absence differs from the normal pattern of absence.

The use of triggers is widespread. About two thirds of the organisations in the IRS (1998) survey used them. They fall into four groups. These need not be mutually exclusive, however, because different sorts of absence may have different triggers for different policy prescriptions. Although the triggers are collectively applied in that they are typically company-, department- or group-wide, it is individuals who usually trip the trigger and to whom the absence policy is applied. This too is not always the case. At Iveco Ford Trucks, breach of the absence trigger giving access to the company sick pay schemes affects the sick pay entitlement of all the relevant employees – even if the trigger is not breached, individual employees may have their entitlement removed if they have been absent sick on two or more occasions amounting to 20 days' absence over the previous 12 months.

The most obvious trigger is one based on *the length of sick leave*, where an absence of over 10 working days might lead to a general review of the individual's record by the line manager and/or personnel department and to a referral to an occupational health service. At Alliance and Leicester Building Society, 10 days' absence over a four-week period leads to a review, whereas Fisons' employees absent for 10 days or longer are referred to the occupational health department (IRS, 1994). A slight variation on this theme is the use of a percentage absence target to determine access to the company sick pay scheme, as at Iveco Ford.

Perhaps more common are triggers based on *the number of spells of absence*. A review might be automatically triggered when an employee is absent x number of times in y months. Practice varies. At Courtaulds European Fibres a computer report is generated after four instances of absence in a 12-month period; five separate instances in the past 12 months at Norwich and Peterborough Building Society; or three absences in a three-month period at Northumberland County Council. These approaches fit more closely with measures of absence based on the 'Bradford factor' (see Chapter 1), where reviews are undertaken once an individual's Bradford points score exceeds certain thresholds. At Vosper Thorneycroft, for example, if an individual's points score exceeds 130, his or her absence may be investigated (IRS, 1994). An early approach used at Rover Group related various stages to the Bradford score over a 52-week period as follows (IDS, 1994b):

Points	Action
200 or more	Recorded formal warning
1,250 or more	Attendance improvement letter (after at least two spells of absence)
3,500 or more	Final attendance improvement letter (after at least two spells of absence)
7,500 and more	Dismissal review

Some organisations use a *combination* of frequency and spells as their triggers – for example, seven days *or* three absences in a 12-month period. The procedure at the Co-operative Bank is to review after 15 days' continuous absence or three spells in a three-month period; Powergen Drakelow use seven days or three absences over the latest 12 months; and Doncaster Metropolitan Borough Council uses 15 days or five separate occasions (IRS, 1994). Royal Mail Scotland and Northern Ireland, as described in the first edition of this book (Evans and Palmer, 1997), had a three-staged approach leading up to and including dismissal:

Stage	Trigger
1	Four absences or 14 days' sick leave in a 12-month period
2	Two absences or 10 days' sick leave in the following six months
3	Two absences or 10 days lost in any six-month period in the 12 months following a Stage 2 warning

Finally, some organisations look for a *pattern* – ie regularly taking off certain days of the week or year. (Such patterns can point to other genuine health problems such as alcohol abuse.) Yorkshire Bank investigates short absences totalling 10 to 15 days, especially where absence precedes or follows weekends.

Whatever triggers are used, they have to be acted on. Royal Mail monitored their absence procedure by analysing whether line managers do actually take action once the triggers are activated.

Absence review and counselling meetings

Absence counselling is an important way of helping employees to identify the causes of absence, any related problems, and how these may be overcome. Counselling interviews are often triggered when certain specified absence criteria have been exceeded. In order to ensure that the criteria are monitored and counselling interviews are carried out consistently, computerised personnel systems are often used to track cumulative absences in a given period and generate 'diary' reminders to personnel staff that action is due. Systems may also have facilities to generate the relevant letter to the supervisor or manager to remind him or her to arrange a counselling interview.

It is important to be clear how a counselling interview differs from a return-to-work interview and from the first stage of the formal disciplinary procedure. The main focus of a return-to-work interview is on the cause of the particular absence in question and, where appropriate, its connections with any pattern of absences that may have been observed, with an emphasis on solving the immediate problem. A counselling interview is likely to be more broad-ranging and take considerably more time than the return-to-work interview, although in practice the difference between the two may not always be clear-cut. Procedurally, counselling often follows a series of return-to-work interviews which have not proved effective in altering the absence behaviour, but clearly precedes the first stage of the disciplinary procedure, which is likely to be invoked if the counselling interview is similarly ineffective. Counselling is not about applying formal disciplinary sanctions, and it is important if it is to be effective that it is not perceived as such. It is about setting aside sufficient time and applying relevant counselling skills. It should also be clearly distinguished from professional counselling, unless the interview is conducted by trained counsellors under the auspices of an 'employee assistance programme'.

The essence of counselling in a workplace is to encourage employees to recognise that there is a problem and to help them come up with a solution which meets the needs of both employer and employee. Following an initial statement of the problem, the emphasis should be on encouraging employees to present their perceptions of the issue and to come up with courses of action that they are prepared to commit to. Effective counselling interviews should not be restricted to a discussion of the immediate issues in hand but encourage a wide focus so that other related or underlying problems can be identified. For example, the cause of frequent short absences may be the result of family, financial or other non-work-related pressures or of problems in the workplace not otherwise apparent. Depending on the resources available to the employer, the result of counselling may be the provision of some further assistance in dealing with the problem. In any event, counselling should result in an agreed action plan to which the supervisor and the employee are committed, which states what further support will be provided (eg training), sets targets for achievement, and makes provision for monitoring and review. The employee should be left in no doubt that any further failure to improve will result in formal disciplinary action, and this, together with the agreed actions, should be confirmed in writing.

Disciplinary procedures

Employers can use a range of formal and informal sanctions against poor attenders. The more draconian of these – disciplinary procedures – feature prominently in surveys of employers' absence-management practices and are covered more fully in Chapter 4.

Using absence as a criterion for redundancy selection

The CBI (2001) found that just over half of all organisations replying to their absence survey used absence as a criterion for redundancy selection in the case of manual workers, and nearly two thirds did so in relation to non-manual workers. This confirms the recent trend away from the traditional 'last in, first out' approach to redundancy and towards the use of multiple criteria for redundancy selection, sometimes based on weighting and scores attached to each criterion (Fowler, 1993; IRS, 1995b). Whereas it would be unusual to use absence as the sole criterion for redundancy selection, IRS (1995b) identified the criteria used by a majority of employers as a combination of skills, performance and attendance. The use of attendance records has the advantage that the information is potentially objective and attendance criteria can be applied consistently. Fowler (1993) cautions that attendance records must be reliable, or there could be a risk of unfair selection, and mitigating circumstances – for example, personal circumstances causing temporary absence problems for employees with previously good records – must be taken into account. Care must be taken to use absence data which, on the one hand, go back a sufficient time period to avoid this situation, but which on the other do not go back so far that historical absence problems are taken into account for redundancy selection even though the problem has long been rectified. Moreover, if any currently long-term sick employees are to be made redundant, industrial tribunals expect the proper procedures, reviewed in Chapter 4, to have been followed. Overall, Fowler advises that attendance should be only one factor in redundancy selection, but recent evidence of organisational practice suggests that it is a factor which is increasingly used.

Policies to encourage attendance

In addition to tackling absence through active policies to discourage it, a range of further measures can help to encourage employees to come to work – measures which have also been linked, as noted in Chapter 2, to high attendance levels and lowered absence. The measures considered here are:

☐ recruitment, selection and induction
☐ flexible working arrangements
☐ job redesign and teamworking
☐ helping with family commitments
☐ occupational health programmes
☐ rehabilitation
☐ rewards for good attendance.

Recruitment, selection and induction

It was noted in Chapter 2 that past absence behaviour – particularly the frequency of absence spells – is a fairly reliable indicator of future absences, and it is therefore sensible to consider what can be done to screen out poor attenders during the recruitment and selection process. According to the CIPD's (2001) absence survey, 44 per cent of employers use previous attendance records as one criterion for recruitment, although very few respondents rated this highly as an effective tool for managing either short- or long-term absence. The CBI's annual absence survey enquires into the use of pre-recruitment medicals as a tool of absence management, and in its 2001 survey over half of respondents used them in this way for manual worker recruitment and three quarters for non-manual recruitment.

The Industrial Society's (1994) study of organisational practices advises that the following measures should be considered:

☐ asking for information about absence on the application form

☐ asking about the number of days lost through absence over the last year or two at the interview (but avoiding or discounting revelations of pregnancy or disability-related absence which may breach discrimination legislation)

☐ asking specifically about attendance levels in a reference request

☐ using 'job previews' to help ensure that all applicants fully understand the job, its pressures and its working environment before they accept

☐ using pre-employment medical screening to focus on any health problems

☐ ensuring that the importance of regular attendance and absence notification procedures are fully explained at induction

☐ closely monitoring attendance levels during a new employee's probationary period.

One organisation which uses pre-employment health questionnaires is Bass Brewers (Arkin, 1997). The screening of the completed questionnaires is carried out on the company's behalf by a specialist health consultancy who advises the company on whether an applicant should have a full examination on the basis of the information provided. In the company's opinion, health screening plays a part in keeping absence levels down, and with absence rates of 2.5 per cent among white-collar staff and 3.5 per cent among manual employees, the company's record compares favourably with the UK average.

A word of caution should be said, however, about the implications of pre-employment health screening in the light of the Disability Discrimination Act (1995). According to employment lawyer Gillian Howard, employers must take care in using pre-employment screening information to reject applicants without enquiring into the reasons underlying any absences reported. If absences relate to disability and an applicant is rejected without further enquiries, this could amount to discrimination under the Disability Discrimination Act. She advises that employers should not use pre-employment screening to reject applicants but rather that applicants should be professionally screened by occupational health physicians who know the exact requirements of the post.

Flexible working arrangements

It was noted in Chapter 2 that absence is affected not just by employees' motivation to attend but by their ability to attend because of family, domestic or travel problems. Now that increasing numbers of employees are combining work and family roles (such as caring for children or elderly relatives), there is some logic in introducing flexibility in working hours or patterns in order to accommodate them. A wide variety of flexible working patterns have emerged in the last 10 to 20 years, and a number of these have relevance for absence control.

Part-time working and job-sharing

Part-time working has been growing significantly in recent years – up from 15 per cent of the total workforce in the early 1970s to 25 per cent today. More than eight of every 10 part-timers are female. Job-sharing is a variation on traditional part-time working which enables a full-time job to be split so that it can be performed by two or more job-holders in a way that the total weekly hours required can be covered by some agreed pattern, such as split days (one job-holder working mornings and the other afternoons), split weeks (one job-holder covering the first part of the week and the other the second) or alternate weeks (Evans and Attew, 1986). According to the Industrial Society's (2002) absence survey, a third of organisations offer job-sharing arrangements, and nearly 40 per cent of respondents rated them as an effective tool of absence management. Similarly, the CIPD (2001) absence survey found that around a third of employers used part-time working and job-sharing arrangements as part of their approach to absence management.

One significant advantage of part-time working and job-sharing is that they more readily enable time to be allocated to work and non-work roles, and consequently less time is taken off during working hours. Absence surveys unfortunately do not provide a very clear picture of whether this is so because they do not provide a breakdown of full- and part-time employees for comparable occupational groups. The CIPD annual absence survey does not provide data by full- and part-time absence, and the CBI's annual survey has not done so since 1997. When the CBI last provided the data, part-time manual absence was higher at 5.1 per cent of time lost than full-time manual at 4.2 per cent, but both part-time and full-time non-manual absence was the same at 3.5 per cent. IRS (1998) found that only 20 per cent of respondents kept data on part-time absence, and that on the basis of the data supplied, part-time absence stood at 2.7 per cent of time lost compared to a full-time absence level of 3 per cent. The Industrial Society's surveys also provide data about full- and part-time absences, and their survey for 2001 found 3.2 per cent of time lost among part-timers compared to 2.8 per cent among full-timers. So although the overall picture is somewhat inconsistent, it does not provide unequivocal support for the proposition that part-time working reduces absence by providing more flexibility to combine work and non-work roles.

Flexitime   *TOIL*

In existence in Britain since the 1960s, flexitime schemes were found by the Gee (1999) survey of absence and attendance practices to operate in around a quarter of organisations. Such schemes usually provide for a fixed number of core hours around which employees have flexibility to vary start and finish times and the length of lunch breaks. They often incorporate facilities for employees to work longer hours if they wish and build up an additional leave allowance that can be used to meet emergencies. Flexitime therefore provides scope for employees to adapt working hours to meet their personal requirements and accumulate a buffer of time off for unexpected contingencies.

All the evidence indicates that flexitime schemes have proved highly effective in reducing absence levels. For example, Dalton and Mesch (1990) found that absence rates fell by about a quarter in the year following the introduction of flexitime amongst one group of employees in an American public utility company, whereas they remained constant amongst employees not receiving the benefit. Moreover, when the scheme was subsequently withdrawn after running for a year, absence levels returned to their former levels. Rhodes and Steers (1990) report a range of studies of the impact of flexitime on absence, almost all of which resulted in lower levels. And more recently, Baltes *et al* (1999) similarly found that flexitime correlated with absence reduction. Gee's (1999) absence survey asked respondents to assess the effectiveness of flexitime in controlling absence and 40 per cent rated it as making 'a major contribution', whereas a further 50 per cent rated it as making some contribution.

Another variant on flexible working hours is the four-and-a-half-day week, finishing at lunchtime on Fridays, which became quite widespread in UK manufacturing industry during the 1980s. Huczynski and Fitzpatrick (1989) report that at one company adopting this approach, Warner Lambert, absence fell by about a quarter, and at another, Baxi Heating, 'significant improvements' were achieved on previous absence levels.

Temporal flexibility

Since the mid-1980s, in addition to the long-established flexi-time schemes, a wide range of flexible working patterns have emerged which are sometimes referred to under the banner of 'temporal flexibility'. In essence, these involve a shift away from the tradition that employment contracts require employees to work a standard number of hours per day and standard number of days per week and towards much greater flexibility of hours which change according to the demands of the business. Depending on exactly how business demands vary, a number of organisations have introduced flexible working hours arrangements whereby hours of work vary by the day, the week or the month according to a predefined pattern, while others have established flexible annual hours arrangements which enable employers to vary hours of work according to demand during the course of a year.

Both the CBI and Industrial Society absence surveys enquire into the extent to which flexible working hours or patterns feature generally and also what role they play in absence reduction. The CBI (2001) found that around 60 per cent of employers operate flexible working practices, whereas the Industrial Society found 40 per cent do so. Over half of the Industrial Society's respondents deemed flexible working hours to be an effective tool for managing absence, and the CBI's respondents also rated it reasonably highly, especially in relation to non-manual staff absence. The Industrial Society (2001) noted that 10 per cent of their respondents used annual hours, although under a quarter described its role in absence management as effective. By contrast, Donkin (1998) reported a fall in absence rates from around 9 or 10 per cent to 3.5 to 5 per cent following the introduction of annual hours working at the Leeds-based dairy food manfacturer MD Foods.

Flexible annual and special leave arrangements

There has been a trend in recent years to move away from granting additional leave for 'special' purposes – such as medical appointments, family sickness or other short-term domestic problems at a manager's discretion – towards for-malising any such entitlement as part of written policy.

Further formalisation of practices in the areas of parental, paternity, adoption and dependant leave have been stimulated by the enactment of a range of statutory rights of employees to special leave since the late 1990s, together with an enhancement of employers' voluntary practices in these areas over and above the statutory minimum (Evans, 1998). As noted in Chapter 2, domestic and family responsibilities can act as a constraint on an employee's ability to attend, even when otherwise motivated to do so. The more such absences become legitimate, either through statutory entitlement or through employers' voluntary policies which enhance the statutory minimum, the less (in theory at least) such absences appear in the employer's statistics of unauthorised or self-certificated absence. Possible links between flexible leave arrangements and absence have been explored by the Industrial Society's surveys. Their 2001 survey indicated that 60 per cent of employers operated these arrangements – up from one third in their 1997 survey – and that half the respondents thought this approach effective in reducing absence. The CIPD's (2001) survey asked specifically about leave for 'family circumstances' and found that over 70 per cent of employers operated such policies, although respondents were more sanguine about their potential role in reducing either short-term or long-term absence.

Working from home

There has been a growth in interest in recent years in the topics of homeworking and 'teleworking' (working from home via a computer terminal linked to the employer's 'host' computer), although it is unclear how many people actually work under such an arrangement. The opportunity to work from home provides the maximum flexibility to organise working time so as to combine work and non-work roles. In principle, it goes a long way towards removing the problems associated with the 'ability to attend' such as travel difficulties, adverse weather problems, the illness of family members or an array of other domestic constraints. Although we know of no study of absence levels among home or teleworkers, it seems likely that this mode of working could potentially be an effective means of reducing absence. Such a view is supported by the absence surveys conducted by Gee (1999) and the Industrial Society (2001). The Gee survey found that 10 per cent of respondent organisations permitted teleworking or home-based working; 20 per cent of respondents using these practices felt that they made a 'major contribution' to absence reduction; and a further 65 per cent felt that they made some contribution. The Industrial Society (2001) found 11 per cent of employers specifically operating the practice of teleworking, and a third of respondents felt that it was effective in reducing absence.

A related development reported by the Industrial Society (2001) is an apparent increase in employers' flexibility to permit employees to work from home occasionally – a policy adopted by nearly a half of employers surveyed, up from a quarter in the 1997 absence survey. Around 40 per cent of the managers who responded to the survey felt that such a policy was also effective in contributing to lower absence levels.

Job redesign and teamworking

The prevailing approach to job design has been broadly based upon the ideas of 'scientific management', but over the past two or three decades alternative models of work design have been offered. Job enrichment, proposed by Herzberg (1966), focused mainly on the redesign of individual jobs and incorporated many of the elements of what today has become generally known as 'empowerment'. Enriched jobs consist of a complete set of related tasks rather than fragmented ones. Greater responsibility and authority for decision-making are delegated to the job-holder, with less close supervision, and opportunities are created for job-holders to learn new skills and perform new tasks. Hackman and Oldham (1975) in a similar vein proposed that jobs should contain the 'core dimensions' of skill variety, autonomy and responsibility for outcomes and feedback on results. Similar proposals were put by the Tavistock Institute (Trist, 1963), but its focus was more on 'autonomous' work groups than on individuals. An autonomous work group should thus experience minimal supervision with devolved responsibility for work standards, be responsible for a complete cycle of activities that result in some meaningful end product (or service), and have opportunities to acquire and use a range of skills and knowledge. More recently there has been a considerable growth in interest in ideas of teamworking, also known as 'high-performance' or 'self-managing' work teams which, according to the CBI (1997), now operate in two thirds of organisations surveyed. These emerged during the 1980s as a central part of organisations' strategies for adapting and surviving in a highly competitive environment, especially, but not exclusively, in manufacturing. Some of the key characteristics of high-performance work groups include (Buchanan in Salaman, 1992, p.148):

☐ multiskilled, flexible work roles

☐ flexible work systems so that skills can be redeployed as required

☐ de-layered management structures

☐ rigorous approaches to recruitment and selection, including the use of psychometric tests and sometimes assessment centres for all employees

☐ encouraging and rewarding the acquisition and deployment of new skills and knowledge, often supported by modular training systems and skills or competence-based pay

☐ a high degree of self-management, minimal supervision and broader spans of control among supervisory and management staff

☐ greater devolvement of responsibility for work methods, work arrangements and quality of output to team level, with a focus on the use of group problem-solving techniques (eg quality circles)

☐ changes in the role of managers from one of close supervision to a more open style, and a greater emphasis on the role of manager as coach, facilitator, mentor and source of advice and support for the team.

In view of the fact that job enrichment, empowerment and

teamworking have a range of potential benefits for organisations, what conclusions can be reached about their impact on absence? In a review of research into the impact of job enrichment generally, Rhodes and Steers (1990) note that nine out of 13 experiments reviewed produced decreases in absence, with a median decrease of 14.5 per cent following the implementation of job enrichment. In studies of job redesign involving autonomous work groups, they found that of the 24 studies that mentioned the level of absence as an outcome, over 80 per cent reported reductions in absence. Where the initiatives involved the development of employees' technical skills, every single study mentioned absence reduction as an outcome.

Rhodes and Steers note in conclusion that of the approaches to job redesign, autonomous work groups are more likely than job enrichment to impact on absence behaviour. This is because autonomous work groups tend to be associated with significant changes in the culture, structure and processes of the organisation. They are characterised by high trust, involve workers in the change process, bring about highly interdependent work roles, and establish clear group objectives and standards. Because absence, particularly in frequent short spells, is likely to disrupt the cohesion of a group in achieving its objectives, individual groups are more likely to develop cultures in which peer pressures are brought to bear on absentees.

The potential role of work groups in enforcing discipline through peer pressure has also been raised by Edwards and Whiston (1989), who observed:

> The rise of 'participation' and 'flexibility' . . . is often seen as implying a disciplinary system in which self-reliance replaces the enforcement of rules. A reasonable further inference is that active policing is no longer needed.

A number of examples of the role of work group discipline in the workplace can be quoted. Peter Wickens, in his book *The Road To Nissan* (1987), notes that the company (in the context of time-keeping) 'has replaced the bureaucratic approach of time clocks with an atmosphere of trust and self-generated discipline within the work group'. If a group

becomes responsible for maintaining good standards of punc-
tuality through peer pressure, why not also good standards of
attendance? Whether connected with group pressure or not,
Nissan is reported in the press as experiencing absence levels
of 3 per cent compared with a UK motor industry norm of 10
per cent.

Similar findings are offered by Drago and Wooden (1992).
They note that there are two possible outcomes from the
existence of strong cohesive work-group norms. Workers
either feel greater loyalty towards each other than to the
firm and engage in anti-firm behaviour – for example, by
establishing high absence norms. Or they feel greater loyalty
to the firm and engage in co-operative behaviour, generating
high commitment and enforcing low absence norms. The
key variables are group cohesion and job satisfaction. Group
cohesion relates to the extent to which group members feel
part of a team and get on well together where the job requires
mutual co-operation. Drago and Wooden (1992, p.776)
conclude:

> Workgroup norms largely control whether absence events
> occur . . . with workgroup cohesion leading to low absence
> where job satisfaction is high and high absence where job
> satisfaction is low.

Other examples may also be cited. Iveco Ford Trucks halved
its absence rate by using peer pressure to stop unwarranted
absence (Arkin, 1993). Boots the Chemists believe that operating small teams of four to five people helps to keep absence
low (Industrial Society, 1994). There is a similar belief in the
value of small teams in controlling absence at IBC Vehicles.
Here, each team consists of six people, with a team leader.
Team members are mutually reliant and cover for each other's
absence. There is also an award for the team that scores the
highest number of points, which are scored for attendance
levels as well as for housekeeping and quality. In terms of
evidence from the various national surveys of absence, the
issue of links between work-group cultures, self-managing
teams and absence levels has been somewhat neglected. The
issue was last explored in the CBI's (1997) absence survey
which identified that two thirds of organisations operated

some form of teamworking which, in the opinion of 70 per cent of the respondents, had proved an effective tool in absence management, constituting a policy rated as having the fourth highest impact on absence levels. We may conclude, therefore, that work-group norms, cultures and the increasing use of self-managing teams with mutually interdependent roles appear to make a significant impact on absence levels.

Helping employees with family commitments

Many of the flexible working arrangements outlined in the sections above recognise one objective to be to work with the grain of employees' family commitments, now widely referred to as 'work–life balance' initiatives. Term-time working, working at home, flexitime, or working hours to fit in with the school day all allow parents better scope to balance their work and their families. Another option is based on providing help with childcare whether on- or off-site. But such arrangements cannot address the problem of caring for sick relatives and the one-off occasional need to take children to the dentist, for example. Evidence of the effectiveness of work–life balance practices in relation to absence reduction comes from a survey of 2,500 employers and 7,500 employees published by the Department for Education and Employment in 2000 (Staines, 2000). Employers rated absence reduction the third most important outcome of the introduction of work–life balance practices. In all, 54 per cent of employers and 58 per cent of employees cited absence reduction as an outcome of work–life balance initiatives.

Occupational health programmes

According to the CIPD's (2001) absence survey, around 60 per cent of respondent organisations involve occupational health professionals in absence management. In addition, a range of further initiatives to support employee health and wellbeing were identified: stress counselling (operated by 32 per cent of respondents); health promotion schemes (28 per cent); rehabilitation programmes (18 per cent); employee assistance programmes (17 per cent); and physiotherapy services (12 per cent). In the views of the respondents, occupational health involvement was seen as the most effective tool for managing long-term sickness, whereas return-to-work interviews were perceived as the most effective approach to short-term absence. The respondents to the CBI's (2001) absence survey ranked occupational health provision as the third most effective initiative for managing non-manual employee absence, and an earlier CBI absence survey in 1998 reported that absence was 20 per cent lower in organisations where an occupational health service was offered and 34 per cent lower where employee counselling was provided.

According to a survey of absence management practices by IRS (1998), two thirds of organisations had access to an occupational health service, and of these, nearly 70 per cent involved its staff in absence management. The roles of occupational health professionals in absence management focused on:

☐ reviewing the cases of individuals with persistent short-term or long-term absences following a referral from line managers or HR staff, usually within the specific provisions of the employer's absence policy or procedures

☐ conducting visits to the homes of employees on long-term sick leave

☐ assisting in the management of the return to work of employees after long-term absence, including conducting fitness-for-work assessments and designing rehabilitation programmes involving alternative duties, locations and working practices

☐ conducting pre-employment medical screening during the recruitment process

☐ providing counselling for employees with sickness absence problems

☐ promoting awareness of lifestyle issues that affect health, including smoking, alcohol consumption and diet.

In conclusion, promoting healthy lifestyles (including smoking and drug abuse policies), retaining occupational health advice accessible to employees, using pre- and post-employment medicals, encouraging a proper attitude to health and safety at work, ergonomically redesigning jobs to reduce physical strains, and ensuring that employees at least have a choice of healthy food in the canteen, are all ongoing strategies employers could use to keep their workforces physically fitter. Keeping them mentally fitter may be more difficult. Job enrichment and empowerment policies help to reduce tedium and raise self-regard, and training employees in stress and time management may help them at least to contain the problem. Employers could also look to flexible working arrangements to help employees balance the competing demands upon them. But probably the biggest change has to come from employers themselves – a change to corporate cultures which recognise the increasing demands being placed on employees, and which seek to do something about them.

Rehabilitation

In the light of the fact that a significant proportion of total time lost through absence is accounted for by long-term sickness, helping employees to get back to work after a prolonged spell of sickness or injury-related absence has to form an important part of an organisation's absence strategy if absence levels and costs are to be tackled effectively. According to the CBI's (2001) absence survey, long-term illness accounts for almost 40 per cent of total time lost through all absence, and other case study evidence suggests that the proportion of time lost through long-term absence may be much higher than this. For example, in the case of Nottinghamshire County Council Social Services reported by Evans (2000), a range of initiatives brought absence down from 11 or 12 per cent to under 7 per cent over three years, but left a hard core of long-term absentees who accounted for 70 per cent of all time lost through absence. Faced with a tightening of the criteria for early retirement through incapacity but also with an objective to bring down absence further, it was recognised that more focus was needed on rehabilitation, redeployment and alternative employment in order to get the long-term sick off the sick-list and back to work. Only in this way could absence levels be brought down to lower levels.

Research suggests that until recently, rehabilitation of the long-term absentee has been very much neglected by many UK employers. In a survey of absence management practices in eight EU countries, Grundemann and van Vuuren (1999) concluded that the main emphasis in the UK had been 'procedural', focusing on monitoring and controlling absence, whereas among many other northern EU members, more emphasis had been placed on an 'integrative' approach. In their view, an integrative approach consists of monitoring and control, taking a range of preventative measures in the area of health and safety management and health promotion, and also incorporates the application of such measures as workplace adaptation, rehabilitation, retraining and redeployment. They note that a requirement for employers to take integrative measures has become enshrined in legislation in Finland, Denmark and Sweden. In another report on return-to-work policies and practices in the UK, IRS (2001) concluded:

> The UK sits at the bottom of the European league table when it comes to getting people back to work after illness and injury. British workers have only a 15 per cent chance of returning to work after a serious injury, compared with a 50 per cent likelihood of return for Swedish workers. UK workplace rehabilitation was recently described as the poor relation of health priorities and employment practice by one government minister.

Research conducted by IRS (2001) into rehabilitation practices in the UK suggests that the picture may recently have begun to change: over 80 per cent of 160 employers surveyed stated that rehabilitation at work had moved up their agendas over the past two years. When it came to questions about practice, however, only 10 per cent had a specific rehabilitation policy, although many others incorporated it in passing in their absence or other policies. A total of 80 per cent of respondents did, however, have a least one employee being rehabilitated back into work after a longer-term sickness absence. In another survey of this issue by James *et al* (2001a, 2001b), just over two thirds of respondents had a written absence policy, but of these, less than half made any reference to contacting longer-term-sick employees to enquire what might be done to facilitate their return to work, and just under a third provided for home visits. Clearly, making contact with the longer-term sick is an important prerequisite of any initiative to understand their problems better and consider what help might be provided to rehabilitate them back to work. Around two thirds of respondents said that they might consider such workplace adjustments as light duties and altered working hours, but only a quarter mentioned the provision of medically supervised rehabilitation. James *et al* also identified a weakness in employer's control mechanisms for monitoring long-term absence. Although three quarters of respondent organisations used 'triggers' (see below) to initiate absence investigations, most of them were based on absence spells in a period designed to pick up short-term, frequent absences, while just over a third of employers based it on length of absence and number of days in a current spell more appropriate for identifying longer-term sickness absentees. On the basis of the findings of James *et al*, the approach of many employers to the long-term sick seems to be one of 'out of sight, out of mind'.

In terms of the elements contained in employers' approaches to rehabilitation, a survey by IRS (2001) identified a rather more positive picture than James *et al*, and identified the following practices on the part of respondent employers:

- phased return to pre-absence duties/hours (90 per of respondents)
- medical examination/review of medical reports (88 per cent)
- maintaining contact with absent employee (88 per cent)
- providing time off to attend medical appointments post-return (84 per cent)
- early intervention to prevent acute conditions becoming chronic – eg physiotherapy, counselling (82 per cent)
- permanently changing or modifying previous tasks (65 per cent)
- providing special equipment/aids (64 per cent)

- ☐ permanently altering pre-absence working pattern (62 per cent)
- ☐ providing retraining (62 per cent)
- ☐ preparation of a return-to-work report (51 per cent)
- ☐ access to private medical treatment (41 per cent)
- ☐ special supervision/mentoring (39 per cent)
- ☐ change of work location (39 per cent)
- ☐ use of internal redeployment register (33 per cent)
- ☐ help with travel to work (28 per cent)
- ☐ providing access to external job placement service (19 per cent).

In terms of the effectiveness of the range of policies available, over half emphasised the importance of early intervention to prevent an acute condition becoming chronic through such services as physiotherapy or counselling; just over a quarter mentioned the importance of maintaining contact; and just under a fifth mentioned a phased return to work. Typically, many organisations require an employee to have been off for at least four weeks before rehabilitation would be made available – perhaps a surprisingly short period. Such a requirement does, however, tend to under-emphasise the importance of early intervention and also the importance of preventative measures. Many rehabilitation programmes, according to IRS (2001), are planned to last over specified periods – ranging typically from four to 12 weeks, with provisions to extend if necessary – and are co-ordinated through a combination of occupational health staff, the line manager and HR staff. In terms of results achieved by rehabilitation initiatives, respondents to the IRS (2001) survey said that three quarters of long-term absentees were able to return to their previous job, a small proportion were redeployed, and, in under 20 per cent of cases, rehabilitation programmes had been unsuccessful and resulted in ill-health retirements or dismissals.

A case example of Marks & Spencer's approach to rehabilitation has been provided by Evans (2000). In the view of the company's chief occupational health physician, rehabilitation not only helps to protect the company's investment in training by retaining experienced staff, to comply with the provisions of the DDA and to create an image of a caring employer, but also enhances the speed of recovery in cases such as depression, chronic fatigue syndrome and back pain. In the case of a pilot initiative designed to provide a phased return to work for staff suffering chronic fatigue syndrome, around 50 per cent were able to resume full hours and duties after six to nine months on the rehabilitation programme, 30 per cent returned and continued on a reduced hours' basis, and 20 per cent declined rehabilitation until their GP had diagnosed a sufficient level of recovery to authorise any return to work.

Rewards for good attendance

Rewards for good attendance take three forms: attendance bonuses, improved sick pay entitlements, and recognition. They all, in their different ways, aim to change employee attitudes to sickness.

Attendance bonus and incentive schemes

Attendance bonuses offend the purists, whose reaction may well be similar to the CBI's view (1989):

> The payment of attendance bonuses is contentious. Some employers have found the payment of bonuses to be a useful management tool. Other companies believe that attendance bonuses can engender a harmful set of attitudes, indicating that the company's requirement for attendance is not integral to the general requirements of employment and can penalise the genuinely sick. Other companies again have found attendance bonuses to have little beneficial effect after the 'novelty' value has worn off. It has also been argued that such schemes may encourage those who are unwell and who should not be at work to report for duty so as not to lose the bonus.

The various published surveys on absence management practices provide inconsistent evidence regarding both the extent of the use of attendance bonuses by UK employers and managerial assessments of their effectiveness. The CBI (2001), for example, found that around 40 per cent of respondents used attendance bonuses for both manual and non-manual staff, compared to between a quarter and a third in their 1999 and 2000 surveys, suggesting growth in their popularity. Despite this, respondents to the CBI surveys in recent years have consistently rated attendance bonuses among the least effective tools for managing absence. Other surveys (IRD, 1998; Gee, 1999; CIPD, 2000; CIPD, 2001) have uncovered much lower uses of attendance bonuses at around 15 per cent of organisations responding, but by contrast have obtained rather more positive responses about their effectiveness in managing absence. In the Gee (1999) survey, for example, around 50 per cent of respondents who used attendance bonuses believed that they made 'a major contribution' to absence reduction. In the CIPD (2001) survey, nearly a quarter of respondents using such bonuses rated them 'the most effective tool' for managing short-term, frequent absences and rated them the third most effective approach from a list of 14 possible tools for managing all types of absence. The real art seems to be in designing a bonus scheme which delivers a payment high enough to affect behaviour, but not too high that its withdrawal seriously affects income, especially for the genuinely sick.

Bonuses can be individual- or group-based, typically paying out every quarter or half year if absence is below a certain level or, in the case of individual bonuses, zero. A number of examples of attendance bonus schemes in practice may be quoted. IRS (1998) reported on a production bonus linked to attendance at furniture-makers Wesley-Barrell. This involved a payment of £25 per quarter to full-time production employees with absence of less than eight hours in a quarterly period. Those with 100-per-cent attendance in a year receive an additional £25 payment. In another bonus scheme at Connex railways (Dunleavy, 1998; IDS, 2001), a quarterly bonus is paid for full attendance, with a further lump sum of £515 if no sickness has occurred during a calendar year. The latter bonus is paid at a reduced rate where there have been up to three days of absence in a year, £105 being deducted from the full £515 for each day of absence up to a maximum of three days. On its introduction, some concerns were expressed by union representatives and employees about the desirability from a health and safety perspective of encouraging staff who may be unwell to attend work, but the scheme has been seen by the company as central to their achievement of a 40-per-cent reduction in absence over a three- to four-year period, and currently 80 per cent of eligible staff qualify for payments. IDS (1998) reported on a range of attendance bonus schemes in seven organisations. Typically, these payments were of the order of £10 to £15 per week; bonuses were normally paid to manual workers on a weekly basis, whereas non-manual attendance bonuses were paid on an annualised basis.

A novel form of attendance incentive operates at Vauxhall Motors (Industrial Society, 2001). For some years, the company has operated a sickness and accident benefit scheme equally funded by employer and employee contributions. As part of the organisation's strategy to bring down absence levels, the employees' contributions to the scheme and the benefits payable have been linked to plant-wide absence targets. Thus, if the absence rate for the plant as a whole (currently 4 to 5 per cent) is not exceeded in the previous 12 months or previous rolling three-month period, the company reimburses all the contributions made by employees at the plant to the sickness and accident benefit scheme. Moreover, where plant absence targets are not exceeded, employees are paid from the first day of absence, without any unpaid waiting days, as provided for in the scheme. Where absence targets for a plant are exceeded, employees contribute their 50 per cent share of the cost of the scheme and have to wait until the third day in any absence spell for sickness payments to commence. The company believes that this approach has contributed significantly to reductions in absence levels from as high as 12 or 13 per cent before its introduction to 5 per cent or less over the period of years in which it has operated. There is a clear danger of paying for attendance twice, but since improved attendance does cut costs, is it fundamentally any different in reward terms from other improvements, such as reduced waste, greater accuracy in processing orders or quicker delivery times? The Rover Group seemed to feel that there was no fundamental difference under the provisions of an attendance improvement scheme operated by the company. There, the scope for employees to earn two half-yearly bonuses recognised the contribution that lower absence made to reduced paybill costs. Payments arose from comparing actual absence levels with a target of zero absence. Starting at the then plant absence rate of 5 per cent, the scheme shared each 1 per cent improvement in absence equally between the company and employees: the employees were able to earn a maximum of 21–22 per cent extra pay for each six-month period. The bonus was earned only by those in full attendance over the period (IDS, 1994).

Such 'gainsharing' approaches are often based on continuous improvement. For example, if absence were reduced to 3 per cent, that becomes the base in the following year, and so on. Consequently, the scope for improvement gets tighter and tighter. Eventually, absence can cease to feature in the gainsharing plan and bonuses switch to achieving other improvements (reduced wastage, health and safety, customer care), although usually in these cases the new reduced level of absence must be maintained if the full bonus from the other source is to be earned. At that stage, pay linked to absence levels stops being a 'carrot' and becomes a 'stick'.

Occupational sick pay schemes

During the last few years more attention has been focused on the role that occupational sick pay schemes can play in helping to reduce absence. There have been three main reasons for this. First, there is the mundane. Some sick-pay schemes actively encourage absence (or, at least, longer periods of absence). One company we know would not pay sick pay for single days of absence but would pay from the first day if absence was longer; the result – a high proportion of two-day absences. Another did not pay the first three days of sickness unless the absence exceeded two weeks; not surprisingly, they found employees tending to take two weeks off to get the full payment.

Second, the introduction of statutory sick pay (SSP) and the subsequent withdrawal of the employers' rebate made employers more cost-conscious. Some chose to reduce the benefits from their own occupational scheme, tighten the eligibility rules, or introduce waiting days.

Third, for many reasons – multiskilling, de-layering, devolution of responsibility, for instance – the trend recently has been to harmonise terms and conditions across the workforce. Treatment under company sick-pay plans was often one of the major differences between blue- and white-collar workers. Bringing in one plan for both offered managers the opportunity to dangle in front of their manual employees the 'carrot' of more generous benefits for lower absence. This was underpinned by a view that if manual employees wanted the same sick-pay scheme as staff, they had to deliver the same (lower) rate of absence.

The Iveco Ford Trucks deal (Arkin, 1993) is a typical example of the *genre*. A high and rising manual absence rate problem was coupled with the need to introduce a new sick pay scheme. Part of the deal agreed with the unions offered the prospect of full payment for the first three days of sickness provided that the plant absence level fell below 3.5 per cent (the white-collar rate) in the previous six months. Although based on a plant-wide target, access to payment from day one is not available to employees if they have been absent on two or more occasions for a total of 20 days over the previous 12 months.

The effect has been beneficial, but the arrangement did highlight a problem – every time absence fell below 3.5 per cent, and employees became eligible for sick pay from day one, the absence rate would rise again. So the rate would yoyo between 3.5 per cent and 5 per cent as access to the sick pay scheme was achieved and lost again. (One answer to this problem might have been to move to an individual rather than a group target.) Borg-Warner Automotive operated a system by which the frequency and length of absence in a year determined the standard of sick-pay scheme the employee would be entitled to in the following year (IRS, 1994). Such an approach has advantages but might weaken the peer-group pressures that keep employees in line.

Another option might be to reduce the 'swing' between three and no waiting days by linking particular absence triggers to different numbers of waiting days – for example, absence at 5 per cent to three waiting days, 4 per cent to two waiting days, 3 per cent to one waiting day, and to no waiting days if absence over a given period is below 3 per cent. This would undoubtedly be complex to operate, but such an approach would smooth out the link between absence rates and waiting days.

In terms of general practices in relation to the use of occupational sick-pay restrictions as a tool of absence management, the CIPD (2001) absence survey revealed that nearly half of all respondent organisations had policies on restricting the sick pay of frequently absent staff, and respondents rated this facility third in a rank order of effectiveness in respect of short-term absence from a list of 18 possible options.

Recognition

Forms of rewarding low absence rates other than cash can also be beneficial. Non-pecuniary rewards include sending letters of appreciation to employees with no absence during a given period, or non-cash prizes such as a dinner or vouchers for goods. Often, non-pecuniary approaches operate alongside other absence policies to reinforce the message that absence does matter to the organisation. IDS (1998) reported on non-cash attendance incentives operating at Oldham NHS Trust. Here, an extra day's annual holiday is granted to employees who have no absences over a 12–month period, and employees with no absences over a period of one, two or three years are also entered into one, two or three prize draws respectively for Air Miles. Food manufacturer Walter Holland & Sons offer a £30 high-street voucher to employees with no absence in a year, a similar £50 voucher to those with no absence in two years, a meal for two at a local restaurant for those with no absence in five years, and a weekend break for two where there has been no absence in 10 years. The awards are presented at an annual ceremony, and at a recent presentation over one third of all staff received some award (IDS, 2001).

Which policies work best?

The $64,000 question at the end of all this is about which absence-control policies work best – that is, which are most effective in reducing absence without, equally crucially, affecting the performance of the business. A policy that bullied a genuinely ill person into attending work and thus spread flu around the office could hardly be considered a roaring success! Similarly, policies that seem unfair to employees by penalising the genuinely sick may be bad for morale and for work attitudes. The defining line between successful and unsuccessful policies can be very fine.

Yet many case studies (including those at the end of this book) demonstrate that organisations adopting absence-management policies and practices which incorporate the measures discussed above *have* managed to bring absence rates down. Some of the more spectacular examples were mentioned in the Introduction – and resulted in reductions of some 50 per cent or more, although some of these improvements occurred over a time-span of some years. Successful absence reduction, however, is often more a matter of using a combination of policies described above rather than relying on one or two alone. Nevertheless, surveys of employers' absence-management practices do indicate that some policies are used more than others, and are felt to be more effective than others.

Absence policies – the employers' view

The CIPD (2001) asked respondents to state which absence management tools were in place in their organisations, and their responses are shown in Table 11.

As is often found in surveys of absence-management practices, the basic building-bricks for most organisations are represented by disciplinary procedures that involve line managers in absence management and provide them with information about absence levels. The use of return-to-work interviews for all absences is also fairly widespread. More recently, the role of leave for family reasons has increasingly been recognised and has risen up the agenda. Increasing too is the involvement of health professionals in absence management, nearly 60 per cent of organisations now making use of this approach. Other health-related measures such as stress counselling, health promotion, employee assistance programmes, physiotherapy services and rehabilitation

Table 11 **THE DISTRIBUTION OF ABSENCE MANAGEMENT TOOLS**

Absence policies and practices	Percentage of respondents using this approach (n = 1,463)
Disciplinary procedure for unacceptable absences	82
Providing line managers with sickness absence information	81
Line management involvement in absence management	78
Leave for family circumstances	71
Return-to-work interviews for all absences	61
Occupational health professional involvement	59
Restricting sick pay	48
Managers trained in absence-handling	44
Attendance record is a recruitment criterion	43
Stress counselling	32
Health promotion	28
Return-to-work interviews for longer-term absences only	20
Rehabilitation programme	18
Employee assistance programme	17
Attendance bonuses or incentives	14
Physiotherapy services	12
Disability leave not counted as sickness absence	10
Nominated absence case manager/management team	7
Others (not specified in questionnaire): home visits	3

Source: CIPD, 2001. p.18

programmes have emerged relatively recently as absence controls used by employers, and it is possible that the significance of these will grow in the future.

The CIPD (2001) also asked respondents about the effectiveness of the tools used, for short-term and long-term absences, and the results are shown in Table 12.

With regard to short-term absences, there was fairly strong agreement that the return-to-work interview was the most useful tool. There was not a good deal of agreement about the effectiveness of the remaining tools for managing short-term absence, although there was reasonable support for the basic building-blocks of absence management – line management involvement, providing line managers with absence information, and the use of disciplinary procedures. When asked about the effectiveness of tools for managing long-term

Table 12 THE MOST EFFECTIVE TOOLS IN MANAGING ABSENCE

Absence policies and practices	Percentage of users who say this is the most effective tool in respect of	
	short-term absence	long-term absence
Disciplinary procedure for unacceptable absences (n = 1,205)	21	9
Providing line managers with sickness information (n = 1,188)	21	8
Line management involvement in absence management (n = 1,137)	31	23
Leave for family circumstances (n = 1,037)	4	1
Return-to-work interviews for all absences (n = 887)	63	17
Occupational health professional involvement (n = 860)	8	64
Restricting sick pay (n = 701)	28	18
Managers trained in absence-handling (n = 650)	14	10
Attendance record is a recruitment criterion (n = 627)	5	2
Stress counselling (n = 464)	2	10
Health promotion (n = 408)	4	7
Return-to-work interviews for longer-term absences only (n = 289)	8	42
Rehabilitation programme (n = 261)	3	39
Employee assistance programme (n = 243)	3	19
Attendance bonuses or incentives (n = 202)	22	5
Physiotherapy services (n = 182)	6	9
Disability leave not counted as sickness absence (n = 143)	0	2
Nominated absence case manager/ Management team (n = 106)	7	36

Source: CIPD, 2001. p.22

absence, almost two thirds saw occupational health involvement as the most effective measure. The use of return-to-work interviews for the long-term sick and rehabilitation programmes also met with some approval.

As noted earlier, no single measure is likely to provide the solution to an absence problem, but the respondents to the CIPD survey provide pointers to those they feel are more effective.

Absence policies – the employees' view

Very little research has been done into employees' attitudes to absence policies and the approaches they think most likely to succeed. More recently employers have started to take account of employee expectations in designing policies, using opinion surveys (see Chapter 5) to find out what really makes the difference in creating an 'attendance' culture, and acting on the results. Other organisations have also gone down the attitude survey route, not only to get employee views on policies but, more importantly, to assess the degree to which employees themselves 'disapprove' of absence levels. Trade unions represent another important conduit of employee discontent – often union officials are only too well aware of absence problems because their members have to cover for absent colleagues and are generally not too happy about it. Employers note that unions rarely have a problem with management's wish to tackle absence, but do want to ensure that policies are fair to their members who are genuinely ill. Many employers, including those in our case studies, have determined absence policies with their employee representatives.

Generally, however, employers often have only a subliminal view of staff attitudes to absence. Most note that staff know who the malingerers are and want the problem dealt with. But few, we suspect, have ever bothered to find out how their employees want to see the issue handled.

Research into employee attitudes to sickness policies carried out by Harvey and Nicholson in 1993 gives some useful pointers. The research was based on a survey of about 1,300 officers in one region of a civil service department. It was built around two fundamental questions asking whether individuals felt there should be (a) an incentive or (b) a penalty to discourage poor attendance. If the answer to either question was 'yes', the respondent was asked to indicate the shape of the incentive or penalty. Individuals were also asked to comment generally on the policies on offer. It is worth noting that as far as penalties were concerned, they thought these should not apply to those genuinely ill; and several opposed incentives on the grounds that attendance was part of what they were paid for already. Moving to the specific, the perceived effectiveness of the two approaches clearly varied with seniority: lower-grade staff tended to favour incentives (although penalties also figured large), but the emphasis given to penalties (and lack of emphasis given to incentives) rose consistently as respondents moved up the grading structure. In terms of each approach, the preferred incentive was a cash award, and the preferred penalty a warning. The authors note that this might imply that the employees individually saw themselves as more likely to earn the award than get a penalty!

Similarly, the preferences varied with age, although of course this also links into grade, in that older people were less likely to favour incentives than young people, and *vice versa* when it came to penalties. This might reflect the fact that other evidence on attendance patterns shows young people prone to take a comparatively high number of short absences, whereas older people are more likely to have one-off breaks for long-term illness. Perhaps younger employees acknowledge that their absences are less legitimate and therefore could be 'bought out', whereas older people are more likely to be genuinely ill, and therefore feel that incentives would be inappropriate. Similarly, older people *know* their young colleagues are swinging the lead and feel they should be penalised, while it would be unfair to treat their genuine illness in the same way.

The authors drew a number of important conclusions about the employees' perceptions of absence policies:

☐ Although employees give a more than expected emphasis

to penalties, they nevertheless do not believe the genuinely ill should be penalised.

☐ Employees would appreciate recognition of good attendance – although it is not clear whether this has to be
tangible or intangible.

☐ Employees have a powerful sense of what is fair.

☐ Measures work best if they have some 'utility' for the
employee; if they are perceived as negative or unfair,
employees may react against them.

Conclusion

Employers have a raft of absence policies at their disposal, and
each one – to some degree and dependent on circumstances –
can help reduce absence levels. Guidelines for implementing
policies are covered in Chapter 5. Four important points from
this review of policies are worth emphasising here. First,
creating an attendance culture is as important, if not more
important, than just setting out to control absence. Second,
line managers are crucial to success but they can't just be left
to get on with it – they must be given training, guidance and
support at all stages. Third, policies seem to work better if
they take account of employee attitudes and needs. Finally,
absence can reflect something else – lax management, boring
work, family difficulties – alongside just illness; find out what
really causes absence in your organisation and you are a long
way towards solving it.

4 THE DISCIPLINARY AND LEGAL FRAMEWORK OF ABSENCE MANAGEMENT

The obligations of employees to attend and the rights of employers to invoke disciplinary sanctions stem from the contract of employment, and the opening part of this chapter therefore takes this as an essential starting-point for considering how absence is to be managed. In particular, employers must consider what their contractual provisions are in relation to attendance standards, and also audit their procedures to ensure that they are fair and comply with the statutory provisions. As part of their review of contractual provisions on standards of attendance some employers have introduced measurable standards, as noted under 'trigger-points' in Chapter 3.

When dealing with absence at the workplace, three important matters have to be considered, and these form the bulk of the remainder of the chapter. The first issue is whether a contract has been 'frustrated' as the result of a long-term sickness absence. The second revolves around the procedures to be followed when attempting to deal with the issue of long-term sickness generally. Finally, the third focuses on the procedures for handling frequent short-term absences.

The contract of employment

The contract of employment sets out the rights, duties and obligations of the employer to the employee and *vice versa*, and the provisions of the contract form the basis on which the effectiveness of an organisation's current absence-control policies should be assessed.

Contractual terms may be either express or implied. Express terms are those actually agreed by the parties and may include collective agreements and works rules. Implied terms are those which may be inferred by the courts or tribunals if not expressly stated by the parties. Implied terms consist of the duties and obligations imposed on the parties by statute, custom and practice (as indicated by the past practices adopted by the parties) and common law. Terms implied by statute are fundamental and cannot be undermined. Thereafter, express terms take precedence over all other sources – ie terms implied by custom and practice and common law (Lewis and Sargeant, 2000). The terms of an employment contract do not have to be specified in writing, but there is a statutory obligation under the Employment Rights Act 1996 to issue written particulars of specified terms and conditions not later than two months after the commencement of continuous employment. There is no statutory requirement as such to provide written particulars of absence procedures or absence management policies. However, related requirements, quite apart from good practice, strongly suggest that an employer should do so in order to clarify exactly what standards are expected.

The statutory requirements related to absence-management policies and procedures are listed below.

First, the written statement must include terms and conditions relating to incapacity for work due to sickness or injury, including any provision for sick pay. This does not imply that an employer must have an occupational sick-pay scheme, since the only legal obligation is to pay statutory sick pay. If, however, an occupational sick-pay scheme applies, details of it must be provided – and where it does not, the written particulars must say so. The details of any occupational sick-pay scheme do not need to be set out in full in the written statement: it is sufficient to refer employees to a separate document which they have a reasonable opportunity of reading. Any changes to the current arrangements must also be notified in writing.

A second requirement impinging upon absence management relates to the statutory obligation to include particulars of any disciplinary rules and procedures applicable to employees, either in full or by reference to another document. Information should include the names or descriptions (eg job titles) of the people to whom employees can apply if dissatisfied with any disciplinary decision and how they should go about this. To the extent, therefore, that absence could become a disciplinary matter (as discussed below), statute requires that the disciplinary framework which would apply must be brought to employees' attention.

It will be evident from the above that two important issues are raised in relation to the employment contract and absence management. First and fundamentally, do our contractual provisions – including associated policies and procedures for absence management – comply with the relevant statutory framework and the ACAS Code of Practice on Disciplinary Practice and Procedures in Employment? Second, do the terms of our contract, whether expressly stated in each contract or specifically referred to by virtue of collective agreements, works rules or staff handbooks, provide a sufficiently clear and unambiguous framework for effective absence management? It is to these issues that we now turn.

The statutory framework and the ACAS Code of Practice

Under the Employment Rights Act (ERA) and subsequent statutes, eligible employees (in the main, employees with one year's service) are entitled not to be unfairly dismissed. When determining unfair dismissal claims, tribunals consider two points:

☐ Has the employer established a potentially fair reason for dismissal?

☐ Did the employer act reasonably in all the circumstances and use proper procedures?

The ERA reaffirms the principle of 'potentially fair' reasons for dismissal, and two of these in particular are of concern when contemplating dismissal as a result of absence. In the case of long-term sickness absence, the potentially fair reason will usually be on the grounds of insufficient capability of the employee to perform the kind of work he or she was employed to do. 'Capability', according to the ERA, is assessed by reference to skill, aptitude, health or any other physical or mental quality, and 'the kind of work' as work which the employee could be required to do under the contract of employment, not just the kind of work actually being performed prior to the sickness absence (IRS, 1995a, p.3). The implication here is that employers are expected to take reasonable steps to find and offer suitable alternative employment either in advance of or in any event following an employee's return from sickness absence if appropriate in the light of the employee's state of health. In the case of persistent short-term absences, on the other hand, the potentially fair reasons for dismissal are likely to be either insufficient capability, where investigation has indicated some underlying medical condition, or misconduct where no medical explanation has been identified. In exceptional circumstances, the potentially fair reason may be 'some other substantial reason' (SOSR). In all circumstances, the onus of proof is on the employer to establish a potentially fair reason – and if that cannot be established, the employer's case will fail. The importance of identifying the correct category of dismissal in relation to absence was highlighted by the case of the *Post Office v Wilson* (1999). In this case Wilson, a postman, had incurred several periods of absence, some of them lengthy, between 1995 and 1997. All absences were for substantiated health-related reasons, but in the latter part of 1997, after a number of warnings had been given, he was dismissed on the grounds of insufficient capability. However, in the face of the evidence that Wilson had no underlying medical condition that was causing his absence and had both been declared fit by his doctor and worked out his notice, the tribunal held that the dismissal was unfair on the grounds stated, given the employee's underlying clean bill of health. The decision was, however, overturned by the Employment Appeal Tribunal who argued that the tribunal should have considered whether the employer had established 'some other substantial reason' for the dismissal. In all the circumstances, noting that the dismissal related neither to conduct nor to capability, the EAT held that SOSR had been established, and found that Wilson had been fairly dismissed. (IDS, 1999; Korn, 1999).

The second issue that tribunals consider is whether the employer acted reasonably or unreasonably in all the circumstances and used proper procedures. When determining this, tribunals take into account 'the size and administrative resources of the employer's undertaking' and make a decision 'in accordance with equity and the substantial merits of the case' (Lewis and Sargeant, 2000). Tribunals are not bound by precedent and may apply different standards to different employers, taking into account the size of the organisation and all the facts before them. In practice, reasonableness includes:

☐ use of proper procedures (as provided for in the ACAS Code [2000a] on Disciplinary and Grievance Procedures)

☐ the consistency of the employer's decision in the light of previous dismissals and disciplinary action

☐ the appropriateness of the dismissal penalty in the light of the offence, the length of service of the employee, his or her previous good record, and any other mitigating circumstances, such as domestic or personal difficulties.

In making their judgement, the tribunals may take the provisions of the ACAS Code into account, and employers who can demonstrate that they have complied with them will be better placed to demonstrate that they have acted reasonably. A useful preliminary step for organisations that wish to tackle absence in a manner which can be demonstrated as reasonable before a tribunal is to audit current disciplinary procedures in the light of the ACAS Code.

However, it is important to note that cases of genuine illness – as distinct from intermittent absences which cannot be explained on health grounds – should not be treated as disciplinary cases. According to the judgement of the Employment Appeal Tribunal (EAT) in the case of *Lynock v Cereal Packaging Ltd* (1988), genuine illness requires employers to treat each case with sympathy, understanding and compassion, while at the same time giving clear indications of the risks to the employee's continued employment should the sickness absence persist (IDS, 1994c, p.21). As indicated later in this chapter, the decisions of tribunals, together with further non-statutory guidance on handling absence contained in the ACAS handbook *Discipline at Work* (2000b), require special procedures to be followed. In the case of longer-term sickness absence, relatively exhaustive processes of enquiry and investigation into the nature of the illness are required, its likely duration and its potential impact on the employee's future employment. Even in the case of persistent shorter spells of absence, certain processes of investigation, although less burdensome, are nevertheless still required.

Express contractual terms and absence management

In addition to outlining an organisation's contractual procedures for handling absence, the express terms of the employment contract – whether specifically within each individual contract or in collective agreements, works rules or staff handbooks – must provide a sufficiently clear and unambiguous framework for absence management (as noted above). This section highlights a range of issues that must be taken into account and documented as express terms of the employment contract.

Essentially, absence management – like all aspects of managing organisational discipline and performance standards – requires a 'control' process. This involves setting the desired standards and measures of performance required, monitoring against the standards set, taking corrective action, and providing follow-up feedback on performance after the corrective action has been taken. The absence-control procedures of many organisations, where they exist, contain elements of this control process but are very often weak on the precise measures of the level of performance required.

The standards set in many organisations focus on *procedural* measures, such as a requirement to notify an absence on the first day by telephone and thereafter to produce the appropriate medical certificates at specified intervals. Many organisations monitor by keeping and disseminating absence statistics, and some also provide for a return-to-work interview, as discussed in previous chapters. Corrective action usually involves the use of the first stage of the disciplinary procedure, or, in some cases, an absence-counselling interview may be held in order to try to achieve some improvement prior to the commencement of formal disciplinary action.

What is lacking in this control process are precise measures of the performance standards required. The result is uncertainty and inconsistency. Many employees have no clear idea of what absence levels will or will not be tolerated, and managers have no clear yardsticks against which to judge what levels of absence constitute grounds for taking either informal or formal disciplinary action. A few organisations have attempted to tackle this by establishing precise measures of what constitute unacceptable or unsatisfactory absence rates and what disciplinary actions will follow from breaches of these standards, and have incorporated these rules as express terms of the employment contract. By setting such precise measures, employers leave staff in no doubt about the attendance standards expected, and help to ensure that absence-control procedures are applied fairly and consistently by managers. These are sometimes referred to as 'absence triggers' and were described in Chapter 3.

When implementing a policy that relies on absence triggers, managements must consider what scope there may be for a joint approach involving the trade unions – and such an approach lies at the heart of the recommendations of ACAS towards disciplinary rule-making. In its handbook on *Discipline at Work* (2000b, p.8), it is recommended that 'management should aim to secure the involvement of employees and any recognised trade unions or other employee representatives when disciplinary procedures are introduced or revised'.

These recommendations reflect its statutory code of practice on Disciplinary and Grievance Procedures (2000a, p.7) which, while recognising the possible reluctance of trade unions to become involved in the matter of disciplinary rules, makes the following proposals regarding the formulation of disciplinary rules and procedures:

If they are to be fully effective, the rules and procedures need to be accepted as reasonable both by those who are to be covered by them and by those who operate them. Management should therefore aim to secure the involvement of workers and where appropriate their representatives and all levels of management when formulating new or revising existing rules and procedures where trade unions are recognised. Trade union officials may, or may not, wish to participate in the formulation of the rules, but they should participate fully with management in agreeing the procedural arrangements which will apply and in seeing that these arrangements are used properly, fairly and consistently.

It is important if absence control is to be effective, therefore, that employment contracts contain rules about objectively measurable standards of attendance, as well as information about the procedural aspects of absence notification and monitoring. Where appropriate, there should be employee and trade union involvement in agreeing the procedures to be followed and, if possible, in defining the measurable standards themselves. However, it must be stressed that a breach of attendance rules alone may not of itself be viewed by a tribunal as justification for dismissal. Tribunals have found dismissals to have been unfair where absence triggers have been applied too rigidly. Employers must still take account of all the surrounding circumstances and operate the rules established reasonably and with due regard for any mitigating factors in each individual case.

The doctrine of 'frustration' and long-term sickness absence

Another issue which may arise out of long-term sickness absence is the question of whether the employment contract has become 'frustrated'. Frustration occurs where events outside the control of the parties make further performance of the contract impossible or radically different from what the parties originally intended. The effect of frustration is to bring to an end the existence of the contract and the obligations of the parties under it. For employees the effect of frustration is that they enjoy no employment protection rights – for example, rights to claim unfair dismissal – since the contract is no longer in existence, having been brought to an end by the process of law. IRS (1995a, p.2) has concluded that as a result of this loss of employment rights 'the tribunals and courts are reluctant to find that frustration has occurred' because of the potentially adverse effect on good industrial relations, and are unlikely to do so unless the employee has little prospect of recovery. It should also be noted that the burden of proof is on the employer to establish that the contract has been frustrated. Key factors to be taken into account when determining whether frustration has occurred include the following, any of which may be considered in an assessment of the overall facts of the case (IDS, 1994c, pp.10–12; IRS, 1995a, pp.2–3):

☐ *The prospect of recovery.* This an important factor and it is unlikely that frustration will be found to have occurred unless the employer has gathered clear medical evidence that an employee has little prospect of recovery. The mere risk of a future deterioration in an employee's health is unlikely to provide sufficient evidence that frustration has occurred. Employers may also be expected to be patient in waiting for a recovery to eventuate. In the case of *Hebden v Forsey and Son*, an absence of nearly two years as a result of an eye operation was not found sufficient to frustrate the contract.

☐ *Length of service.* As will be described further below in the context of sickness absence dismissals, employers are generally expected to be more patient in awaiting the return of a longer-serving employee.

☐ *Expected future duration of employment* if sickness absence were not a factor. This takes into account the temporary or permanent nature of the employment and whether it was likely to have come to an end irrespective of the sickness absence.

☐ *The employer's need for the work to be done.* This factor focuses on the extent to which the absent employee's skills and knowledge are readily replaceable. If they can be replaced by another employee, the employer can be expected to wait longer than if the skills and knowledge cannot so readily be replaced and a new appointment becomes necessary. For example, in the case of *Hunt v A.*

R. Marshall and Sons, a tribunal held that an employer could not be expected to continue with temporary arrangements after the absence of a key worker for four months.

☐ *The nature of the job.* Employers are expected to assess the potential impact of the illness on the employee's ability to perform the job or a reasonable alternative job in the future before frustration can be considered to have occurred.

☐ *The risk that the employer might acquire employment protection obligations towards a replacement employee.* In assessing whether a contract might be frustrated, employers are entitled to take into account redundancy or unfair dismissal rights that would accrue to replacement employees after the requisite period of service.

☐ *Whether the employee has gone on being paid.* Where an employer continues to pay wages or sick pay or to make continued payments to an employee's pension fund, it may constitute evidence that the employer wishes to maintain the contractual relationship. It should be noted, on the other hand, that the mere exhaustion of occupational sick-pay entitlement will not of itself permit the employer to consider the contract at an end. Employers' practices with regard to occupational sick pay vary enormously, given that there is no obligation to pay more than statutory sick pay. Practices can vary from the provision of no occupational sick-pay scheme, as is the case in nearly half of private sector employers (particularly smaller ones), to up to one year's pay in the case of some large employers (IDS, 1991, p.7; IDS, 1994b, p.9). The vicissitudes of employers' sick-pay policies thus mean that exhaustion of entitlement provides no conclusive evidence of frustration.

☐ *The acts and statements of the employer in relation to the employment.* The nature of frustration is that the ending of the contract does not require a formal act of dismissal since the contract has come to an end by the process of law. In cases of frustration, the courts and tribunals may nevertheless be interested to understand why there was no formal dismissal.

In the final analysis, the courts and tribunals will weigh up whether a reasonable employer can be expected to wait any longer for the employee to return. However, as IDS (1994c) conclude, 'Employers should be cautious in invoking the doctrine of frustration,' and Cox (1999) has similarly concluded that 'It is advisable for employers not to rely on the doctrine of frustration, but rather to expressly terminate the employee's contract after following a fair procedure.'

A number of cases of frustration have nevertheless been upheld by the courts in the context of long-term absence. In *Jones v Secretary of State for Employment* (1996) it was held that a driver and labourer with 15 years' service who had developed back problems resulting in an absence of 22 months could not successfully claim redundancy pay because his contract had been frustrated by his long-term inability to perform his duties (Croner, 1999). In *GF Sharp and Co Ltd v McMillan* (1998) it was held that the contract had been frustrated when a serious hand injury rendered McMillan, a joiner, permanently incapable of performing his duties (Croner, 1999). By contrast, in the case of *Williams v Watson's Luxury Coaches* (1996) it was held that the contract had not been frustrated after Ms Williams, a typist with five and a half years' service, had been absent for 19 months due to a non-permanent injury, eight of these months being uncertified absence before returning to work (Croner, 1999). This latter case illustrates the importance of weighing the factors, listed above, which may be considered in cases of frustration. In this case, there had been a recovery and a return to work and the employee was not seen as a key worker whose skills were difficult to replace.

It is recommended that where frustration is invoked, employers should be prepared to plead an alternative defence – namely, that there was a dismissal for a potentially fair reason on the grounds of the employee's incapability through long-term sickness. Such a defence requires a fair procedure for handling long-term sickness, and it is to this topic that we shall now turn.

Long-term sickness procedures

As we noted at the beginning of the chapter, the burden of proof lies with the employer to demonstrate that a dismissal arising out of long-term sickness is for a potentially fair reason – and, in the case of genuine illness, this relates to the employee's lack of capability to do the kind of work he or she was employed to do or any alternative work of a broadly similar nature he or she might reasonably be expected to do. As well as establishing a potentially fair reason for dismissal, employers must also demonstrate that they acted reasonably and applied a fair and proper procedure.

General guidance on this is contained in the ACAS code on Disciplinary and Grievance Procedures (2000a). In the case of dismissals arising out of long-term absence, further guidance is available regarding the fair procedures that must be followed.

The first source of these is the ACAS handbook *Discipline at Work* (2000b, pp.40–45), which presents an authoritative but non-statutory view. The non-statutory nature of the ACAS handbook was emphasised in the case of *British Coal Corporation v Bowers* (1994) when the Employment Appeals Tribunal (EAT) reminded tribunals that it did not have the legal status of a statutory code of practice (IRS, 1995a). The second source of guidance emanates from the decisions of the courts and tribunals in long-term sickness absence cases. In addition, all the factors noted above in relation to frustration will also be considered in assessing the reasonableness of the dismissal, taking into account all the relevant facts in the circumstances of each individual case.

The remainder of this section considers each of the recommendations made by the ACAS handbook regarding the handling of long-term absence, adding guidance where available from relevant cases. A fair procedure for handling the dismissal of long-term sick employees consists of three elements (IDS, 1994c):

☐ consultation with the employee
☐ medical investigation
☐ consideration, where appropriate, of alternative employment before dismissing.

In addition, three further issues that arise out of long-term sickness dismissals must be taken into account, and these are:

☐ the impact of providing permanent health insurance
☐ the impact of the Disability Discrimination Act (1995)
☐ absence related to pregnancy or maternity leave.

Each of these will be considered in turn.

Consultation with the employee

The ACAS handbook (2000b, pp.42–43) provides the following advice:

> The employee should be contacted periodically during the period of sickness absence and in turn should maintain regular contact with the employer.

> The employee should be kept fully informed if employment is at risk.

> Where the employee's job can no longer be kept open and no suitable alternative work is available, the employee should be informed of the likelihood of dismissal.

> Where dismissal action is taken, the employee should be given the period of notice to which he or she is entitled and informed of any right of appeal.

It is important to note that this process involves genuine consultation and two-way communication in order to establish the true medical position. According to the EAT, consultation has two purposes: to ensure that the situation has been properly weighed up, balancing the employer's need for the work to be done against the employee's need for time to recover; and to ensure that steps are taken to establish the true medical position (IDS, 1994c).

It is also important that genuine illness is treated with sympathy and understanding, not as misconduct on the part of the employee. The EAT has stated that 'warnings' are generally inappropriate in these circumstances and could even be damaging to the employee's recovery. However, warnings might become appropriate in certain circumstances where an employee exacerbates the situation by refusing to follow medical advice. Examples here include refusing to follow a diet to control obesity or refusing to undergo a simple operation which would restore fitness for work. Although warnings are generally inappropriate (except in such circumstances), the employer must nevertheless inform the employee if his or her continued employment is at risk, following the ACAS (2000b) recommendations. The difference is one of nuance and emphasis, and – as IRS have concluded (1995a) – 'At the end of the day, tribunals will generally be more concerned with the procedures followed than with the labels given to those procedures.'

A failure to consult the employee is generally fatal to an employer's case if dismissal action is taken. As Phillips J. stated in the case of *East Lindsey District Council v Daubney* (1977), 'If the employee is not consulted and given the opportunity to state his case, an injustice may be done' (IDS, 1994c, p.13). In this case the employers were found to have unfairly dismissed an employee on the basis of their own doctor's report, which in turn had been based on an examination carried out by another doctor. The employee had not been given an opportunity to state his case or to obtain an independent medical opinion.

According to IDS (1994c), proper consultation with the employee should include four specific points:

□ Discussions should take place in the early stages of the illness and periodically throughout its duration, and the employer should give clear indications when the duration of the illness has begun to put the employee's future employment at risk. Following the recommendations of the ACAS handbook (2000b), the employee should be informed when the decision to dismiss has been taken, should be given the period of notice to which he or she is entitled, and should be informed of any right of appeal.

□ The employer should make personal contact before dismissal – ie the decision to dismiss must have been preceded by face-to-face contact and not have been conducted by post or on the telephone.

□ The employer must give due consideration to the employee's opinions on his or her condition: this requires employers to take account of the employee's views on the likely date of return and about the work he or she would feel capable of performing on his or her return. However, employers must balance the employee's own assessment with that of professional medical opinion (as discussed below). The dismissal of an employee on the basis of a personal assessment of health alone is likely to be unfair. In the case of *Jones v Nightfreight (Holdings) Ltd* (1988), the employer relied on the employee's own assessment of the date when he thought he would be well enough to return, and when the employee failed to turn up on that date he was dismissed. The dismissal was found to be unfair on the grounds that the employer over-relied on the employee's own assessment at the expense of obtaining professional medical opinion (IDS, 1994c).

☐ The employer must give due consideration to possible alternative work should the employee prove unable to return to his or her former duties. (This will be considered further below.)

There have been very few exceptions to the general principle that failure to consult is likely to render a dismissal for long-term sickness unfair (IDS, 1994c). In the case of *Taylorplan Catering (Scotland) Ltd v McInally* (1980), the employee had suffered long-term sickness as a result of depression caused by working in an isolated environment in the Shetland Islands. The employee was subsequently dismissed without consultation. The employers took the view that consultation would have been pointless in that they could not alter the environment which had caused the illness. The EAT agreed, arguing that the purpose of consultation was to help an employee over the problem and get back to work – outcomes which were highly unlikely in this case. In another case, *Eclipse Blinds Ltd v Wright* (1992), the employee's health had deteriorated to a point which made return to work unlikely, a fact confirmed by her GP to the employer. Her GP had decided not to disclose her true medical condition and she believed she was getting better. In these circumstances, the employer dismissed without consultation for fear of disclosing the true position inadvertently, and the court held that the employer had not acted unreasonably in these specific circumstances.

Medical investigation

The general position is that employers must take steps to find out about the employee's true medical position, and that a failure to seek medical advice, where this is appropriate, is likely to result in a finding of unfair dismissal. The employer is therefore required to seek medical advice from an employee's GP or specialist, probably also from the company physician, if there is one, and sometimes to obtain the views of an independent specialist.

ACAS (2000b) summarises the steps which employers should take in order to obtain medical information about employees as follows:

Before applying to an employee's doctor for a medical report, the employer must notify the employee in writing that it is proposed to make the application, and must secure the employee's consent in writing.

In addition, the employer must inform the individual that he or she has

☐ the right to withhold consent to the application's being made
☐ the right to state that he or she wishes to have access to the report
☐ rights concerning access to the report before (or after) it is supplied
☐ the right to withhold consent to the report's being supplied to the employer
☐ the right to request amendments to the report.

Where an employee states that he or she wishes to have access to the report, the employer must let the GP know this when making the application and at the same time let the employee know that the report has been requested.

A letter of enquiry [see ACAS, 2000b], approved by the British Medical Association, may be used and the employee's permission should be attached to the letter.

The employee must contact the GP within 21 days of the date of the application to make arrangements to see the report; otherwise, his or her rights will be lost.

If the employee considers the report to be incorrect, he or she may make a written request to the GP to make appropriate amendments.

If the GP refuses, the employee has the right to ask the GP to attach a statement to the report reflecting the employee's view on any matters of disagreement.

The employee may withhold consent to the report's being supplied to the employer.

On the basis of the GP's report the employer should consider whether alternative work is available.

Where there is reasonable doubt about the nature of the illness or the injury, the employee should be asked if he or she would agree to be examined by a doctor to be appointed by the company.

Where an employee refuses to co-operate in providing medical evidence or to undergo an independent medical examination, the employee should be told in writing that a decision will be taken on the basis of the information available and that it could result in dismissal.

Where an employee is allergic to a product used in the workplace, the employer should consider remedial action or a transfer to alternative work.

The 'rights' to which ACAS is referring emanate from the Access to Medical Reports Act (1988) and the Access to Health Records Act (1990). The Access to Medical Reports Act gives individuals some specifically defined rights in relation to medical reports relating to them which are supplied by medical practitioners for employment purposes. The Act defines a 'medical report' as a report prepared by medical practitioners responsible for the clinical care of the individual (IRS, 1995a). This definition is therefore likely to exclude reports prepared by company doctors or independent specialists who are not responsible for the clinical care of the individual.

The Act requires employers to notify employees of their wish to approach their personal physician for a medical report, to obtain the employee's consent to make the application, and to inform the employee of his or her rights under the Act. These rights include giving consent for the application to the personal physician to be made and for a report to be supplied; the right to see and agree the contents before it is supplied; and the right to request alterations or amendments before it is supplied. If the employee's physician does not accept the need for any proposed alterations or amendments, the employee has the right to append his or her comments before it is supplied. The employee's right of access to the report can only be limited or denied where a doctor believes that disclosure could be potentially damaging to the patient's physical or mental health. It is important to stress that the employee ultimately has the right to withhold consent for a medical report to be supplied, but any refusal to co-operate in this way has implications which are discussed below.

In respect of the procedure to be followed to obtain consent, employers should write to the employee seeking consent to approach the personal physician for a medical report, inform the employee of his or her rights, and obtain written acknowledgement and agreement to all the contents of the letter. The next step is to write to the personal physician (see ACAS, 2000b, p.90 for an example letter), attaching the employee's consent.

The Access to Health Records Act (1990), which came into force on 1 November 1991, gives individuals the right of access to 'health records' made by any health professional responsible for care after that date. The distinction between this and the 1988 Act is that the latter refers to 'reports' by a personal physician and the former to 'records' created by any health professional. Employers may, with the employee's consent, also obtain access to his or her medical records.

Some issues arise out of specific cases and have implications for the application of the procedures recommended by ACAS.

The first point of contact is usually the employee's GP, who should be asked about the nature of the illness, the expected period of absence and the type of work the employee will be capable of on return to work, subject to the employee's consent to make such enquiries (IDS, 1994c). In return, the employer should give the GP (or any specialist) information about the nature of the employee's work, the reasons for the enquiry and the risks (if any) to the employee's future employment (IRS, 1995a). Employers should not, however, rely solely on the diagnosis of the GP as stated on the medical certificate or in any report supplied or from any other correspondence. In the case of *Crampton v Dacorum Motors Ltd* (1975), the employer dismissed a service manager aged 50 on the basis of the GP's diagnosis of angina, having made some further informal enquiries about the nature of this condition. The dismissal was held to be unfair on the grounds that in such circumstances employers must take reasonable steps to discover all the relevant facts, which should have involved further examination by a specialist identified either by the employee's physician or by the company (IDS, 1994c; IRS, 1995a).

Another issue may arise where employers have sought and obtained a second medical opinion – for example, from their own company doctor – which differs from, say, that of the employee's GP or the specialist. If the employers decide to dismiss on the basis of one of these reports, they will need in principle to show reasonable grounds for preferring one medical opinion over another. Yet there are some indications from existing cases that the views of employers' medical advisers may carry more weight because of their greater knowledge of the job and working environment. This applied in *Ford Motor Company v Nawaz* (1987), where the EAT held that employers could not be expected to weigh up conflicting medical opinion and had acted reasonably in dismissing on the basis of their own medical advisers' opinions (IRS, 1995).

Ultimately, as the EAT has stated, the decision to dismiss is not a medical question but an employment question, taken in the light of the available medical advice (IDS, 1994c). However, the employers may still run the risk that they have dismissed without a thorough investigation of all the facts. In the case of *British Gas plc v Breeze*, the opinion of the employer's medical adviser conflicted with that of the employee's GP, who held the view that the employee would be able to return to his job. The company's medical adviser recommended that a third, independent opinion should be sought, but this was not taken up. It was held that the dismissal was unfair on the grounds that more information should have been sought (IDS, 1994c). So while there appears to be some conflict between these decisions, employers may well be advised to obtain a third opinion where the first two opinions differ.

A third issue which may arise concerns an employee's refusal to consent to a medical examination or to the disclosure of a medical report or medical records. An employer cannot force an employee to undergo a medical examination, unless that has been provided for in the contract, and cannot in any event gain access to a medical report or medical records without the employee's consent. Provided that the employer has taken reasonable steps to secure the employee's co-operation in gathering medical evidence, but has failed to do so, the employer is then entitled to take action on the basis of the evidence available, even if that falls short of revealing the full medical position. This means that a dismissal may be held to be fair even if medical evidence, had it been available, might have indicated to the contrary (IDS, 1994c). This was the position in the case of *McIntosh v John Brown Engineering* (1990), where a dismissal was found to be fair following an employee's refusal to allow a report to be given to the employer by his GP, or to be examined by a company doctor or an independent specialist (IDS, 1994c). Employers must, however, have followed the consultative process described earlier and have taken all reasonable steps to obtain medical evidence.

Whatever the issues regarding medical evidence, the EAT has recognised that the decision to dismiss a long-term sick employee is not a medical but a management issue. According to IRS (1995a), the process of consulting the employee and medical opinion should produce sufficient information for the employer to provide answers to the following questions:

☐   Is the employee likely to make a full recovery, and if so, how long will it take? Can the employer reasonably be expected to keep the employee's job open until he or she is fit to return to work?

☐   If the employee is not going to recover completely, what will be the extent of his or her continuing disability? Will this affect the employee's ability to do the job which he or she was employed to do?

☐   If it is likely that the employee will only recover sufficiently to resume work in some different capacity, is it possible to offer some alternative employment on his or her return from sickness absence?

It is to this last question that we now turn.

Alternative employment

The ACAS handbook (2000b, p.43) provides the following brief guidance:

> On the basis of the GP's report the employer should consider whether alternative work is available.
>   The employer is not expected to create a special job for the employee concerned, nor to be a medical expert, but to take action on the basis of the medical evidence.

Evidence from tribunal and court cases strongly indicates that a failure to consider alternative employment properly, as distinct from considering it but finding nothing suitable, is likely to render a dismissal unfair. A number of cases illustrate the point. In *Dick v Boots the Chemists Ltd* (1991), the dismissal of a store detective after three years' absence was held by the EAT to have been unfair, even though a doctor's report stated that she would never be fit to perform her job again. The company's procedure had been seriously flawed by failing to consider alternative employment even in these circumstances (IDS, 1994c; IRS, 1995a). As IDS (1994c, p.24) concluded, it is clear that seeking and, where possible, offering alternative employment is fundamental to a fair dismissal in long-term sickness cases.

Various decisions also indicate that an employer, though not expected to create a job, must take a flexible approach and consider what assistance could be provided in order to make a suitable offer of alternative employment. Decisions in various cases have included:

☐ a willingness to accept someone back on a part-time basis

☐ a willingness to accept someone on day work, even though the job was only performed in shifts

☐ a willingness to reorganise a job so that, for example, less heavy lifting was required

☐ a willingness to transfer an employee to other tasks – for example, where an allergy has prevented the performance of former ones.

The impact of providing permanent health insurance

A number of employers provide permanent health insurance (PHI), which makes payments to employees who suffer a breakdown in health that prevents them from continuing in their current or similar work. These payments are likely to continue until recovery, death or retirement, and some schemes require that the recipients of PHI benefit remain employees. Depending on the exact rules of the scheme, there will usually be some qualifying period of absence before any payments are made. The case of *Aspden v Webbs Poultry and Meat (Holdings) Ltd* (1996) highlighted the care to be exercised by employers when dismissing a long-term sick employee with contractual rights to permanent health insurance. In this case, Aspden's contract entitled him to PHI after 26 weeks' incapacity, subject to his meeting the qualifying conditions, one of which was being an employee. The benefit was thus not available if he was dismissed. His employment contract also provided for dismissal on grounds of ill-health following three months on full pay and three months on half-pay. In the event, Aspden was dismissed, losing his rights to PHI. The court decided that where there is a contractual right to PHI and the terms of the scheme require an applicant to be an employee, an employer cannot dismiss on health grounds – unless there are grounds for summary dismissal – and deprive an employee of these rights. The effect of this ruling is to make it difficult to dismiss an employee contractually covered by PHI where continued employment is a requirement of the scheme. In the case of *Villella v MFI Furniture Centres Ltd* (1999), an employee had been in receipt of PHI payments when the insurer withdrew them on the basis of medical evidence. The employers continued to make payments from their own pocket, but in due course ended these payments also and dismissed the employee. The employee sued for payment, arguing that his termination did not bring his entitlement to PHI payments to an end. In this instance, the insurance policy between the employer and the insurers had contained a restriction that benefits would not be payable to someone who had left employment, but no such clause had been incorporated into the employee's contract of employment nor had he been told about it. The contract had merely stated that the benefit would cease on the employee's return to work, or on attainment of age 65 or on death, whichever occurred first, and thus it was held that the employee was entitled to continued payments (MacDonald, 2001).

Olga Aiken has suggested that in such situations it would be sensible to replace an employee's original employment contract with a new one when an employee transfers to PHI for the sole purpose of paying the benefit or, alternatively, to agree with the insurer at the time of taking out the policy that employment can be terminated and the payment will be made direct by the insurer to the employee (Aiken, 1996a, 1996b).

The impact of the Disability Discrimination Act (1995)

The Disability Discrimination Act (DDA) came into effect in December 1996 and embodies the rights of people who have 'a physical or mental impairment' which has a 'substantial' and 'long-term adverse effect' on the ability of an employee to carry out 'normal day-to-day activities' (CCH, 1997). A 'long-term effect' is one which has lasted at least 12 months or is expected to last that period. The Act protects an employee who is disabled within the above definition from discrimination in all aspects of employment, including recruitment, promotion, transfer, training and dismissal. Discrimination is defined as the treatment (by an employer) of a disabled person less favourably than others who are not disabled, without justification. It is also discriminatory for employers to fail to make 'reasonable adjustments' to either their premises or to their employment arrangements – such as working hours – where a failure to do so would cause a substantial disadvantage to a disabled person, subject to the resources available to the individual employer.

The key issues regarding the dismissal of a long-term sick

employee who may fall within the definition of a disabled person for the purposes of the Act are as follows. First, even if an employee has not suffered 'impairment' for at least 12 months and not been absent for that period, he or she may be protected if medical opinion considers that it is likely to last that long. Second, it is important to bear in mind the definition of discrimination, as set out above. To discriminate, the employer must treat the employee 'less favourably' than others without a disability within the definition of the Act. It is essential, therefore, that employers treat all long-term sickness cases – whether or not they could be defined as disabled under the Act – in the same way, and demonstrate that no one is treated more or less favourably. If this is done, long-term sickness dismissals should not be deemed unfair within the meaning of the Act. Third, however, employers must bear in mind the obligation to make 'reasonable adjustments' to the workplace or working arrangements in order to help alleviate disadvantages faced by a disabled person compared with others who are not disabled. It would, therefore, be discriminatory to refuse to implement such adjustments in order to allow a long-term sick employee who has recovered sufficiently to return to work. It would also be discriminatory to refuse to allow a return to work on the grounds that the employee is likely to lose too many days through absence. The only circumstances that permit less favourable treatment occur where the employee genuinely cannot do the job for which he or she was employed or any other job that might reasonably be offered, or where reasonable adjustments to the workplace are either impracticable or demonstrably beyond the resources available to the employer or where the nature of the disability significantly impedes the performance of the duties (CCH, 1997).

The types of 'reasonable adjustments' that employers might be required to consider include the following (IDS, 1999; Employers' Forum on Disability, 2000):

☐ making physical adjustments to the workplace
☐ allocating some of the disabled person's duties to another person

☐ transferring the disabled person to another vacant post, with or without reasonable adjustments being made

☐ altering the disabled person's working hours, possibly encompassing part-time working, job-sharing or other flexible hours arrangements

☐ providing special equipment to assist the disabled person to perform his or her tasks, and giving training in the use of the equipment

☐ retraining the disabled person to perform an alternative role

☐ allowing full or partial working from home

☐ allowing time off to attend medical appointments, treatment or rehabilitation.

When considering what reasonable adjustments may be appropriate in each specific set of circumstances, it is advisable to obtain expert advice beyond, for example, that of a GP acting as the company doctor. Sources of expert advice include Disability Employment Advisers, contactable through local Job Centres (who can also advise on any financial asssistance available through the Access to Work Scheme), specialist doctors or occupational health physicians.

Although case law under the DDA is still evolving, some examples of tribunal cases heard provide useful illustrations, and a number revolve around the issue of 'reasonable adjustments'. In the following cases, applicants brought successful actions. The case of *Kerrigan v Rover Group Ltd* (1997) illustrates that reasonable adjustments involve taking a more flexible approach to employees with disabilities compared to those who are able-bodied when operating attendance-improvement initiatives. In this case, the employee suffered from asthma, which caused frequent absences and prevented him from achieving the standards required by an attendance-improvement scheme. Faced with the possibility of dismissal through early retirement on grounds of incapacity, the employee brought an action to a tribunal. The tribunal, finding in his favour, held that reasonable adjustments should have been made to the attendance-improvement scheme in his case in order to prevent him from being placed at a substantial disadvantage (IRS, 1999). In the case of *London Borough of Hillingdon v Morgan*, Ms Morgan's medical adviser had recommended a gradual return to work on a part-time basis following ME. The employer was, however, unable to offer such an arrangement and so dismissed her. The tribunal held that considering part-time working would have been an appropriate and reasonable adjustment to have made, all the more so as the employer had implemented such flexible arrangements as redeployment and working from home for other staff (Employers' Forum on Disability, 2000). In the case of *Tarling v Wisdom Toothbrushes Ltd*, the company was given medical advice that Ms Tarling, a disabled employee who had experienced ongoing absence problems and difficulties in meeting production targets, might better be able to perform her duties using a specially designed chair costing £1,000. The chair was also available on a free trial and financial assistance for its purchase might have reduced the net cost to the employer to £200. The employer failed to pursue this and so a tribunal hearing held that the purchase of the chair would have been a reasonable adjustment to have made and upheld the employee's claim for discrimination on grounds of disability (Hall, 1998). In the case of *Cox v Post Office* (1997), the employers put forward the defence that a postman who had incurred excessive absence as a result of asthma had impeded their ability to offer an efficient service to their customers, this being a legitimate line of defence under the DDA. The defence failed on the grounds that the employers were unable to offer evidence of any costs actually incurred or to give any specific examples of disruption to their business (CCH, 2000).

Cases in which applicants' claims have been unsuccessful include the following. The case of *Arboshe v East London Bus and Coach Company* illustrates the importance of offering alternative employment as a possible response in meeting the employer's duty to make reasonable adjustments. The employee was a bus driver whose driving licence had been revoked after he had been diagnosed with insulin-dependent diabetes. The employer offered two alternative posts, a clerical job and a bus conductor's job. Arboshe felt that he could not perform either of these roles, turned them down, and the employer dismissed. The tribunal rejected the applicant's claim on the grounds that potentially suitable alternative posts had been offered, even though they entailed a cut in salary (Employers' Forum on Disability, 2000). The case of *Wood v Daron Motors* (1997) illustrates other aspects of 'reasonable adjustments' as part of the employer's defence. In this case Wood, a motor mechanic, had undergone an amputation of his right leg following a car crash. The employer held his job open for a number of months while he recovered. Wood returned to work for a few months before the condition of his leg deteriorated and he went off sick again. The company tried to find out when he would be fit to resume work, but medical opinion was inconclusive, and the employee was dismissed. At the ensuing tribunal it was held that the employee was disabled within the meaning of the DDA, but that no discrimination had taken place because the employer had implemented reasonable adjustments, including holding the employee's job open, allowing him time off for recovery and giving him additional time off when at work to attend hospital treatment. Moreover, the employer had attempted to obtain a medical assessment, but in the absence of specific information had reached a reasonable decision to dismiss in the light of an assessment of the position (Goldman and Lewis, 1999). In the case of *Clarke v Novacold* (1997), Clarke was dismissed for sickness absence which related to his disability. He had been absent for five months after suffering a back injury at work and was dismissed. The employer had obtained a medical report which said that his condition should improve over a 12-month period, but gave no firm indication of when he might return. Following a tribunal hearing, it was held that Clarke had been treated in the same way as any other employee on long-term sick leave and had therefore not been treated any less favourably than staff without disabilities (Hargreaves *et al*, 1998).

Absence related to pregnancy or maternity leave

Great care must be taken when dealing with sickness absence during pregnancy since the law sets down that a pregnant woman may not be subjected to detriment, directly or indirectly, on grounds of pregnancy. In the case of *Brown v Rentokil* (1998), the employer operated a strict policy of dismissal after 26 weeks of continuous absence. Brown had been off continuously for this period with pregnancy-related illnesses and the employer dismissed in line with the policy. When the employee took the matter to a tribunal, the employer's decision to dismiss was upheld, as it continued to be during further appeal stages, on the grounds that the woman had not suffered detriment since a male employee off 26 weeks would have been treated similarly. The matter eventually went to the European Court of Justice which overturned the decision, holding that since men cannot become pregnant, the comparison with male employees was irrelevant and concluding that the unfavourable treatment amounted to direct sex discrimination. The decision confirmed that any dismissal arising out of pregnancy will be automatically unfair. However, special provisions exist under the Maternity and Paternity Regulations (1999) regarding pregnancy-related sickness absence occurring where the employee has elected to continue to work after the sixth week before the expected week of childbirth. If an employee goes absent for a pregnancy-related reason in this period, the employer may trigger the commencement of maternity leave automatically.

As regards sickness at the end of the maternity leave period, where an employee has given notice of her intention to return on a specific date but fails to do so and instead reports in sick, the employer must wait until she is well enough to return (as an employer would be expected to do in the case of any employee unable to return on a previously agreed date after sickness absence because of continuing ill-health). Because the employment contract remains in force during maternity leave until the employee gives notice of an intention not to return, the employer should apply the contractual terms and sickness arrangements – such as the payment of SSP or occupational sick pay (if applicable) – in the normal way. This approach was confirmed in the case of *Halfpenny v GE Systems* (1999), in which the Court of Appeal held that an employer's dismissal of an employee who failed to return from maternity leave on an agreed date was unfair on the grounds that a right to return existed once the employee had given notice of her intention to do so.

Moreover, if an employee has returned from maternity leave but continues to incur absences related to pregnancy or childbirth, any dismissals related to these absences are likely to be seen as automatically unfair, even if they continue for a period of time after her return. This was confirmed in the case of *Caledonian Bureau Investment and Property v Caffrey* (1998), where the Employment Appeal Tribunal held that a dismissal arising out of pregnancy-related absences some time after return from maternity leave constituted both unfair dismissal and sex discrimination (MacDonald, 2001; Lewis and Sargeant, 2000).

Procedures for dealing with persistent short-term absentees

Whereas in many organisations longer-term sickness accounts for the majority of the time lost through all absence, persistent short-term absence for apparently unconnected reasons (such as colds, flu, headaches, etc) is difficult to plan for and disruptive to efficient operations. Both the ACAS handbook (2000b) and various principles arising out of the case-precedents provide employers with guidance on procedures to be followed.

An essential starting-point is a full and proper investigation of the facts in order to try to establish the causes of the absences. If some underlying medical explanation is uncovered, the procedure for dealing with genuine sickness absence – as described above – should be followed. Ultimately, if there is no resolution to the sickness problem, any dismissal will be on the grounds of insufficient capability. If, on the other hand, no medical explanation can be discovered, then any dismissal is likely to be on the grounds of misconduct arising out of the employee's poor attendance record. It is essential that employers establish on the basis of investigations which of these two diagnoses is applicable, since the procedure to be followed – and the reason for dismissal – is different. Where no underlying medical explanation can be found to account for frequent, short-term absences, the matter is likely to be treated as minor misconduct and will normally require the use of all four stages of the disciplinary procedure set out in the ACAS Code on Disciplinary and Grievance Procedures – which are:

☐ oral warning

☐ first written warning

☐ final written warning

☐ dismissal.

Before an oral warning is issued at the first formal stage, the ACAS Code also recommends that the matter is discussed informally in the first instance at a counselling or absence-review meeting. It is also important to note that the employee has the right to be accompanied in the formal disciplinary stages, and an absolute right to appeal after any warning has been issued to a higher authority, whether or not any new evidence is to be offered. A further important point to note when tackling frequent short-term absences is the required existence of clear rules and standards, as discussed above. However, as is always the situation when dismissing, the wider circumstances of each case must be taken into consideration. Such factors will include the employee's past attendance record, any mitigating personal or domestic problems, and the likelihood that the employee's attendance record will improve in the future. So although the attendance rules may contain clear trigger-points (as described in Chapter 3) for which certain disciplinary consequences have been specified, breach of these rules alone may not be sufficient to justify dismissal when the surrounding circumstances are taken into account.

The remainder of this section provides guidance on the procedures to be followed in the case of frequent and persistent short-term absenteeism. The ACAS handbook (2000b, pp.41–42) is a useful starting-point and recommends that the following processes should be followed:

☐ Absences should be investigated promptly, and the employee asked to give an explanation.

☐ When there is no medical advice to support frequent self-certificated absences, the employee should be asked to consult a doctor to establish whether medical treatment is necessary and whether the underlying reason for absence is work-related.

☐ If after investigation it appears that there were no good reasons for the absences, the matter should be dealt with under the disciplinary procedure.

☐ Where absences arise from temporary domestic problems, in deciding appropriate action the employer should consider whether an improvement in attendance is likely.

☐ In all cases the employee should be told what improvement in attendance is expected, and warned of the likely consequences if it does not happen.

☐ If there is no improvement, the employee's age, length of service, performance, the likelihood of a change in attendance, the availability of alternative work, and the effect of past and future absences on the business should all be taken into account in deciding appropriate action.

ACAS concludes its advice as follows (2000b, p.42):

> It is essential that the persistent absence is dealt with promptly, firmly and consistently in order to show both the employee concerned and other employees that absence is regarded as a serious matter and may result in dismissal. An examination of records will identify those employees who are regularly absent, and may show an absence pattern. In such cases employers should make sufficient enquiries to determine whether the absence is because of genuine illness or for other reasons.

The ACAS guidelines reflect good industrial relations practice, as does the guidance provided by the tribunals and the EAT. An important case was *International Sports Company Ltd v Thompson* (1980), in which the EAT elaborated on the procedures which employers ought to follow in cases of frequent short-term absence (IDS, 1994c, p.19; IDS, 1994a, p.9). The key steps identified are:

☐ a fair review by the employer of the employee's attendance record and reasons for the absences

□ an opportunity for the employee to make representations

□ appropriate warnings of dismissal if the situation does not improve.

The EAT concluded that if there was no adequate improvement in the attendance record after this procedure, dismissal would be justifiable (IDS, 1994c).

Each of the above steps will now be examined in turn.

The starting-point is the use of return-to-work interviews after each spell of absence, with brief notes taken during the discussions. If the pattern of short-term absences persists thereafter, there should be a further investigation of the individual's overall absence patterns, days lost and reasons given for each spell of absence. This requires the keeping of absence statistics and, ideally, a computerised system that automatically generates a report when specified absence triggers are passed or specified patterns are identified (eg patterns of Friday or Monday absences). In the case of a first offence, a meeting should be called with the employee to discuss the facts and seek more information. Depending on the procedure, such a meeting may in the first instance consist of an informal counselling discussion or form part of the formal disciplinary procedure. It is important that no assumptions or prejudgements are made about the nature of these absences, and the key priority must be to identify whether there might be an underlying medical explanation or whether other personal or domestic circumstances are causing the absences. In the case of frequent, short-term and apparently unconnected absences, the EAT has held that there is no absolute requirement to produce medical evidence or to contact the employee's GP, unlike the requirement applying to longer-term sickness absences.

Nevertheless, it would be wise for an employer to attempt to do so in order to demonstrate that reasonable attempts have been made to uncover some underlying explanation. For example, in the case of *Smith v Van Den Berghs and Jurgens Ltd* (1991) the employer was found to have unfairly dismissed an employee for misconduct due to his absenteeism for which no medical evidence had been sought. Medical evidence was subsequently presented to the tribunal by the employee and it was concluded that the absences were for genuine reasons (IDS, 1994c).

Where an employee's absences are mainly self-certificated, it would be appropriate for an employer to propose and seek an employee's consent to a medical examination. If an underlying medical explanation is uncovered, the procedures considered in the previous section for sickness absence should be followed. Equally, if the process of investigation and consultation reveals some personal or domestic problems, the employer should take note of them and the employee's views on how he or she is attempting to solve them. The employee should be allowed time to implement a proposed plan of action, and the situation should be kept under review.

Where no underlying medical explanation nor any other mitigating circumstances can be identified, continuing short-term absences should be dealt with through the disciplinary procedure. This will involve the use of warnings and possibly also the setting of attendance targets to be achieved. In the final analysis, an employer is entitled to conclude that 'enough is enough'; where employers have investigated the facts, explored the possibility of a medical or other explanation, consulted the employee regularly about the level of absence and followed the disciplinary procedure laid down, any ensuing dismissal is likely to be fair.

The key is establishing a fair reason on the basis of the facts and the discussions, and acting by applying a fair procedure.

As well as considering the individual circumstances of the employee concerned, the employer is entitled to weigh up the impact of the absences on other staff and on the efficiency of the organisation as a whole. When dismissal is being contemplated, therefore, the EAT has suggested that employers must ultimately consider the following factors which will be relevant to their tribunal evidence:

□ the nature of any illness, if applicable
□ the likelihood that further absences may occur
□ the length and frequency of the absences and the periods of attendance between them

- ☐ the need of the employer for the work to be done by a particular employee
- ☐ the impact of the absences on other employees
- ☐ the adoption and exercise of fair and consistent absence policies and procedures
- ☐ whether the employee's personal assessment has been taken into account in the ultimate decision
- ☐ the extent to which the difficulty of the situation and the position of the employer have been explained to the employee.

PART II

PUTTING TOGETHER AN EFFECTIVE ABSENCE-CONTROL STRATEGY

5   MEASURING THE ABSENCE PROBLEM

During the course of this book we have so far considered a number of perspectives on the management of absence: its measurement, its causes, its control, and the importance of auditing organisational practices in the light of legal requirements. *The next three chapters of this book are designed to provide the reader with a systematic and practical framework for the effective management of absence* within his or her own organisation.

As we indicated in Chapter 1, the nature and causes of employee absence are highly variable, typically reflecting a diverse mix of individual and organisational factors. It follows, therefore, that there is no simple 'off-the-shelf' solution to resolving absence problems, at either the individual or the organisational level. At the organisational level, absence levels may be influenced by a wide range of potential factors, such as working environment, job design, culture, management style, pay and location. At the individual level, each employee and every instance of absence will undoubtedly be different. In practice, the reasons for individual absence range from genuine and unavoidable illness through to straightforward malingering, but, as always, the majority fall into the uncertain and often highly problematic grey area between these two extremes.

Against this background it is not possible or desirable to offer any kind of universal panacea. The development and implementation of any absence management programme must be customised to the specific needs of the organisation in question. It must be based on a clear and reliable understanding of the actual dynamics that are influencing absence levels across the organisation as a whole and perhaps also within specific locations or work-groups. It must comprise a mix and level of provisions – cultural, environmental, procedural and perhaps financial – appropriate to the characteristics that have been identified.

In other words, you need to be sure that you are addressing, as precisely and fully as possible, the factors that will really make a difference in your particular organisation. Without such careful targeting, the programme is likely to be less than effective and may even prove counter-productive, particularly in the longer term. For example, if the primary causes of absence in the organisation are environmental, then a relatively punitive approach, with a substantial focus on, say, on the withholding of sick pay or application of disciplinary processes, may bring immediate improvements but merely exacerbate the problem in the longer term. Conversely, if absence levels are largely the product of ineffective line management or weak procedures, then the most urgent requirement will be to address these shortcomings. If that is not done, the adoption of more supportive approaches to absence management may be perceived merely as legitimising current practices.

In developing an absence management programme it is critical to apply a systematic approach which starts from a thorough diagnosis of the current characteristics and needs of the organisation. *In this final section of the book, therefore, we provide a comprehensive framework for identifying and responding to the requirements of your organisation.* The key stages are:

1   measuring and costing the current absence problem
2   benchmarking and setting targets for achievement
3   analysing the causes of absence
4   analysing the effectiveness of current approaches to absence control
5   planning and implementing an absence-control programme
6   monitoring and evaluating its effectiveness.

In the remainder of this chapter we look at the first two key stages – collecting, collating and analysing the data needed to assess our requirements, and developing our objectives for future improvement.

Measuring and costing the current absence problem

In crude terms, the first question to ask is 'Do we have a problem?' In practice, of course, it is not possible or even desirable to eliminate employee absence entirely. The majority of employees at some stage suffer from some genuine sickness or other legitimate incapacity. Although this still presents an unfortunate cost to the organisation, it is generally preferable – both for themselves and the employer – that employees take appropriate sickness absence in such circumstances. An employee who feels obliged, for financial or other reasons, to attend work while genuinely ill risks both exacerbating his or her own condition and, if the illness is infectious, potentially spreading it to colleagues. In both cases the resultant costs may substantially outweigh any theoretical savings achieved by the original attendance!

In developing our absence management policies, we therefore need to ensure that we are addressing inappropriate and unacceptable absence, while not being unduly coercive to those who have genuine reasons for non-attendance. More generally, we also need to ensure that our proposed investment in managing the absence problem is proportionate to the costs that are currently being incurred by employee non-attendance. There is no doubt that – as noted in Chapter 1 – the costs of absence are generally substantial (and usually underestimated). Nevertheless, there may be little point in investing heavily in absence management if, in reality, our absence levels are already relatively low and are unlikely to be further reduced by management intervention. Similarly, it may not be necessary to invest in substantial organisation-wide activities if, in truth, any absence problems are concentrated in specific locations or work-groups, reflecting perhaps local environment or management factors that could be resolved more directly.

It is essential then for us to begin by making sure that we have accurate information about the level and characteristics of absence within the organisation, so that we can begin to assess the size and nature of the problems we are facing. As described in Chapter 1, the key basic information required is time lost, frequency of absence instances, and absence costs. (With such data, and a broad target for absence-reduction plans – eg from an average of 10 days per annum per employee to eight days – it is also possible to make useful estimates of the likely savings you will be able to generate, as shown in the calculations set out in Chapter 1.) The need for such information may seem obvious, but it is surprising how many organisations have failed to establish even basic data collection procedures, according to various surveys of absence management practices.

The challenges of collecting and analysing absence data

The monitoring of levels and costs of absence appears to have improved in recent years, according to evidence drawn from the annual CBI absence surveys and similar sources. Nevertheless, it is clear that many organisations still do not keep complete records of time lost by staff, and that data on absence costs is still relatively limited and incomplete. For example, although 71 per cent of respondents to the CBI's 2000 survey were able to provide an estimate of direct absence costs, the CBI reported that:

> the survey also asked employers to report on the indirect costs of absence – reductions in quality or service, etc – but so few were able to put a value on this cost that the data cannot be used to extrapolate to the UK as a whole.

Yet where respondents did provide an estimate of indirect costs, it typically amounted to three or four times the direct cost. It is also worth bearing in mind that in this area the CBI sample is likely to be partly self-selecting – employers are less likely to respond to the survey if they lack reasonable absence data! The CIPD survey *Employee Absence* published in May 2000 reported that only 41 per cent of respondents monitored the cost of sickness absence, while only around 20 per cent monitored the indirect costs of reduced performance.

Although the statistics vary, therefore, the available evidence strongly suggests that many organisations still fall at the first hurdle of developing an effective programme for absence control – that is, they simply do not have the required information. Without such information it is impossible to carry out external benchmarking of current performance, to set targets for future performance, or to analyse costs. To put it another way, such organisations cannot even say for certain whether they have a 'problem' with absence, let alone assess the scale or nature of that problem or identify the steps required to resolve it!

In many respects, the common failure to gather even basic absence data is surprising. After all, in most organisations, there will already be established processes for collecting data on individual absences – both for local supervisory and resourcing purposes and to inform occupational or statutory sick-pay schemes. As a minimum, employees will be required to report absence, provide medical certificates, and so on. All too often, however, this individual data remains at local level and no effort is made to aggregate it into departmental or organisational statistics. In practice, therefore, the preparation of at least high-level absence statistics should be a relatively straightforward task for most organisations, requiring simply the collation and analysis of data which, in some form, is already being gathered.

The failure to analyse the cost of absence is perhaps more worrying, since it implies that many HR departments are unable to talk the language of costs – the 'lingua franca' of businesses and organisations – in discussing absence issues. Considerations of the cost of absence are a fundamental building-block of any absence-control initiative, defining both the scale and size of the initiative and its perceived value and credibility among senior management. Clearly, any credible absence-control programme must be based on a clear and measurable assessment of the current costs of absence, the likely costs of the programme itself, and the expected financial benefits that will accrue from the implementation of the programme. Without such information, it is unlikely that any proposals will be seriously entertained. Where such information is available, the potential benefits of effective absence management are very often self-evident – typically a demonstrable and substantial contribution to the 'bottom-line' performance of the organisation. In truth, although operational management generally perceives employee absence as an irritation and inconvenience, its real costs are often severely underestimated. It is commonly perceived primarily as a 'human resource' problem rather than as a direct and significant driver of business performance. Our case study of James Cropper plc in Appendix 1 at the back of this book provides a striking illustration of the potential impact that improved absence management can have on business performance, since management calculated that every 1 per cent improvement in attendance levels was worth approximately £100,000 in reduced costs.

As we have already noted, many organisations simply do not collect the raw data from which they can calculate the costs of absence – that is, they do not know, in aggregate form, how many employees are absent, for what periods, or with what frequency. However, even where such statistics are available, many report that they are still unable to calculate absence costs, typically citing the time and difficulty involved in processing the data.

According to the CIPD's survey of employee absence (2000), around 80 per cent of respondents indicated that they used computerised HR information systems to perform the calculations on their absence data; such systems were used by over 60 per cent even of those employing fewer than 100 employees. This suggests that there has been a substantial expansion in the use of computerised HR systems in recent years (the 1997 Industrial Society survey of absence management practices reported only around a third of respondents using such systems). This is likely to be a positive trend. Gathering and costing absence data manually is potentially very time-consuming. We would therefore suggest that in all but the smallest organisations some computerised system of absence recording and reporting is likely to be a prerequisite of any effective absence-control programme. Where no computerised HR information system exists, it is probable that the investment in a system would be more than justified by the potential for cost savings as a result of more effective absence monitoring through computerisation. As we have noted, even in an organisation of 500 people the cost of absence could be of the order of *£500,000 a year*, not counting the indirect costs of overstaffing, temporary workers, over-time or disruptions to workflow (Evans, 1991). In its 1993 survey, the CBI found that organisations which relied on manual record-keeping for absence control had 16 per cent higher absenteeism than organisations that kept computer-ised records. This suggests that for any relatively large organisation the potential benefits of more effective absence management might justify investment in an appropriate HR information system, even discounting the wider benefits available from computerising HR data.

Even where a computerised HR information system is in place, it may be necessary to assess whether the system is sufficiently sophisticated and flexible to provide the data required. In most cases where some computerised absence-recording facility is available on the system, it will be capable of counting days lost by individual, grade, department or other variables, although some systems cannot calculate the fre-quency or number of absence spells. More commonly, systems may not be capable of effectively supporting the costing of absence because they do not hold data on hours of work or average pay, which may be stored separately on payroll systems. If links between the two systems are unavail-able, it may prove necessary to transfer or analyse the cost data manually or by downloading data into a spreadsheet or similar package for calculation purposes.

Ideally, an effective computer system ought to be capable of providing an integrated absence-warning system. Such a system, as was described in earlier chapters, can be pro-grammed to generate warnings to system users or line managers when certain absence thresholds or triggers are exceeded, and help to ensure that appropriate follow-up action takes place on a consistent basis. Some systems will, for instance, provide an automatic calculation of the 'Bradford factor' (described in Chapter 1), or similar formula, which can be used to trigger warnings at pre-specified levels.

In short, then, the fundamental building-block of an effec-tive absence-control programme is complete and accurate information. Effective absence-reporting procedures ensure that each absence is accurately recorded in the first place and held on computer for the purpose of analysis. The computer system itself has to be sufficiently flexible so that all the statistics required can be calculated, including time lost, frequency of absence spell and absence costs. Ideally, systems should also be able to generate warnings to help ensure that effective follow-up action is taken in every case. Where human resource professionals are working with existing systems which may not offer the required range of facilities or flexibility, it will be necessary to develop support mechanisms, based either on manual calculation or on the downloading of data into more specialised software, to ensure that appropriate data is available. Where new systems are being specified or introduced, care will be required to ensure that the system really can provide the appropriate links and outputs – for example, making links between absence and pay data or ensuring that data can be analysed against the required organisational variables.

Benchmarking and setting targets for achievement

Benchmarking best practice has now become widespread in British industry, practised by at least two thirds of organisations (Syrett, 1993). It is essentially concerned with making statistical comparisons of performance with other organisations and assessing whether the performance measures in a specified organisation are better or worse. Where they are worse, benchmarking can be used to establish targets for achievement in the future, as well as to help identify potential changes in practice and approach that may be necessary or helpful to achieve these targets. However, the CIPD survey of employee absence (2000) indicates that only around a third of respondents benchmark their absence performance against other employers' (although the figure is much higher in some sectors, such as local and central government and health).

In an article in *People Management* (June 1997) Alan Fowler suggested that effective benchmarking involves the following activities:

☐ identifying the performance improvement area to be

studied in terms of measurable criteria in order to make comparisons with other organisations

☐ choosing relevant organisations with which to make comparisons

☐ studying benchmarking data to identify possible opportunities for improvement

☐ using benchmarking data to examine the procedures of the best-performing organisations in order to pick up ideas that can be adopted or adapted to achieve improvements.

We look at each of these activities in turn.

Identifying the performance improvement area to be studied

In order to make comparisons with other organisations it is essential to identify the performance improvement area to be studied in terms of measurable criteria. In the case of absence, the relevant criteria require adequate data using the standardised measures discussed above – time lost, frequency, and cost for each relevant employee category, eg manual or non-manual, occupational group, location, etc. Care must be taken to ensure that appropriate criteria and variables are selected. For example, if we believe it would be helpful to distinguish between manual and non-manual staff, we have to consider how these categories should be defined and then ensure that our definitions appropriately reflect those used in the organisations with which we are benchmarking. We also need to ensure that we have identified sufficient variables to provide meaningful data on the nature and potential causes of absence in the organisation. For example, we may wish to compare data relating to particular occupational groups, particular geographical areas, particular contractual groups (such as staff working part-time or on 'unsocial' shift patterns), or some combinations of these.

Choosing relevant organisations with which to make comparisons

Obvious initial sources of comparative data are the surveys conducted regularly by the CBI and the Industrial Society. However, it should be recognised that nationally-gathered data of this kind has limitations. These surveys provide general absence data by industry sector, occupational group, geographical region and organisational size, but not all of these in a single analysis.

If, for example, we wished to benchmark absence rates of systems analysts and programmers in a software company in central London employing 1,000 people, the national surveys will provide only highly approximate information for benchmarking purposes. In practice, comparisons based on discrete single variables may be misleading – our absence levels may compare favourably with other central London organisations or with software companies nationally, but still be relatively poor compared with similar companies locally. Moreover, the data provided are sometimes based on averages, whereas when benchmarking we may wish to identify the best performer or an upper-quartile performer and not wish to content ourselves with performing at the industry average. In this context, it should be noted that the CBI absence survey provides information on upper- and lower-quartile absences by industrial sector.

For more precise benchmarking information it is necessary to target organisations with which we wish to compare ourselves. These may include competitors, organisations working in related but non-competitive fields, or organisations recognised as setting high standards of performance. Such an approach is most commonly based on participation in benchmarking 'clubs', either run by consultancies or established on a voluntary basis by the organisations themselves. It is common to find such benchmarking clubs operating within a given geographical area or within specific industries or sectors, such as financial services, IT or parts of the public sector. In establishing or joining the benchmarking group, however, it is critical to ensure that you are gathering comparative data which is appropriate and meaningful. It is not unusual to find that superficial similarities actually mask significant differences that may potentially distort comparisons.

At a simple level, you will have to ensure that all parties are calculating absence levels on the same basis. This may be a particular consideration if, for instance, your calculations include time lost from non-standard or variable working patterns, such as annualised hours arrangements. You should ensure that the relevant employee categories and other variables have been defined in the same way. You may also wish to explore in detail the respective characteristics and employee profiles of comparator organisations. It is possible that apparently similar organisations may actually have quite different structures or profiles which might significantly affect absence levels – for instance, varying levels of staff on short-term contracts, different proportions of management/non-management staff, substantially different age-profiles, and so on. These differences do not necessarily invalidate the benchmark comparisons (and they may, indeed, help you to identify potential solutions to your absence difficulties), but they must be understood if you are to interpret the statistical benchmark data appropriately.

Studying benchmarking data to identify possible opportunities for improvement

Having identified an appropriate comparator group, you can then use the benchmark data to help identify your problem areas and to inform your targets for improvement. Typically, your first step should be to match your absence levels with the relevant average rates among the benchmark group – this will help to indicate the nature and extent of any absence problems within your organisation and help you to prioritise your responses. For example, it might be that your absence levels for both operational and management staff are running at, say, 5 per cent. If the benchmark comparisons show average absence levels of 6 per cent among operational staff but only 2 per cent among managers, you may decide that your absence levels for operational staff are tolerable – but that you need to address management absence as a priority. You might also find that apparently high absence levels are in fact relatively standard for a particular industry or particular occupational group. This does not of course mean that there is no scope for absence levels to be improved, but it does enable you to target your responses realistically and cost-efficiently. If you are addressing a group where absence levels are already below the benchmark average, you may have to recognise that relatively high levels of investment may bring only limited returns, because some of the causal factors may be intrinsic to the nature of the group or its environment. At the same time, although average rates provide a valuable guideline for prioritisation, organisations that are ambitious for significant performance improvements may wish to target themselves to match the best rather than the average performer in the benchmark group.

Overall, therefore, you must ensure that any targets are realistic, given the relevant benchmark data and your desired level of investment in addressing the issues. To inform such judgements, you will have also to ensure that benchmarking data is available for relevant comparable groups. The absence targets set for, say, senior managers, clerical staff and manual workers may well be different, and it might also be appropriate to establish different targets for various occupational or other employment groups, depending on factors such as working conditions or environment, nature of contract, location, and so on.

In practice, this raises an important management dilemma – the extent to which it is acceptable to set variable targets for absence rates, and, indeed, the extent to which it is appropriate to publish targets at all. In most organisations, the formal position is that no unplanned absence is desirable, and that the 'ideal' absence target is zero or close to zero (acknowledging that, as discussed earlier in this chapter, a level of genuine absence is likely to be unavoidable). The setting of any target, however carefully presented, implies an 'acceptable' level of absence which more cynical employees might be tempted to treat as a norm. The application of more sophisticated formulae, such as the 'Bradford factor' (described in Chapter 1), helps to reduce this risk but does not remove it entirely. In one organisation that used the 'Bradford factor' as the basis for triggering formal absence procedures, there was evidence of employees' planning their future absence in order to remain inside the trigger levels! This risk may be exacerbated if, on the basis of benchmark data, differential targets are set for respective employee groups. Is it acceptable, for instance, to set a less demanding target for, say, operational staff than for senior managers, simply because this is the existing norm elsewhere?

There is no simple solution to this dilemma. One option is not to publish any aggregate targets at all but simply to use such targets, within human resources and the senior management group, as the basis for prioritising activity, allocating resources and evaluating progress. This reduces the risk that the targets might be abused – but reduces the opportunity to communicate to staff the scale of the requirement and the organisation's progress towards meeting it. If they are used effectively, such targets can provide a valuable prompt and incentive to staff to improve their collective attendance levels. Moreover, even if the targets themselves are not published, it is likely that, as part of the absence-management programme, they will inform trigger levels for taking action on individual absence records. These trigger-points will have to be published, resulting in the same risk of abuse.

A more constructive approach may be to recognise that even if the ideal is zero, ambitious attendance targets will not be achieved overnight. It may be more appropriate, therefore, to take on board the idea of continuous improvement, setting year-by-year targets to be achieved by departmental managers that bring absence levels down progressively over a period of time. This enables the organisation to reflect the existing absence levels, both internally and among the benchmark group, while also asserting that the ultimate target should be both highly ambitious and consistent for all groups. In other words, the ultimate standard for existing problem groups is equally demanding, but there is an acknowledgement that it may take longer to reach this ideal level in areas where absence is currently running at a higher level. The case studies in this book demonstrate that bringing absence rates down significantly can take a number of years. Both James Cropper plc and the Scottish Prison Service have adopted progressive targets to drive continuing improvements in attendance.

Examining the procedures of the best performers to pick up ideas
Benchmarking is very much concerned with performance measures, but effective benchmarking also offers substantial

further benefits. Systematic benchmarking also involves the sharing of information practices and experiences within the participating benchmark companies. This might, for instance, involve sharing data about the nature and apparent causes of absence, about the steps that have been taken to achieve absence reductions, about the effectiveness or otherwise of specific policy initiatives, and about any practical difficulties that had to be overcome.

The application of benchmarking to inform absence management programmes is likely to be most effective if there is meaningful, qualitative sharing of information between the participants rather than merely an exchange of statistical data. First, as indicated above, it is helpful to have an understanding of the characteristics of the various organisations, in terms of factors such as location, types of roles, working environment, workforce profile (in terms of age, length of service, and so on), contractual terms and conditions, and relative salary levels. Although it may not be possible to obtain details of all this information, an investigation of these factors may be highly illuminating in helping to identify the potential causes of absence and possible solutions for your organisation. By examining the apparent areas of similarity and difference between organisations, it may be possible to begin to isolate those factors that are most influential on absence levels. If, for instance, there are substantial variations in absence levels among apparently similar categories of staff, you may then wish to explore other potential contributory factors, such as environmental or employment conditions.

Benchmarking can often also be a powerful tool for questioning or challenging existing organisational assumptions or practices. Managers in your organisation may have become accustomed to high absence levels, either simply because these have traditionally been the norm or perhaps because the organisation is perceived to be operating in a 'difficult' environment with challenging working conditions or high stress levels. They may therefore initially be reluctant to invest in any significant absence-management programme, believing that it will be difficult to achieve any significant impact on absence levels. If it is possible to provide examples of broadly similar organisations with much lower absence levels or to demonstrate instances where equivalent organisations have achieved significant improvements in attendance levels, this often provides a valuable lever for change. The example of the Scottish Prison Service, one of the case studies in this book, provides a very impressive demonstration of how substantial improvements can be achieved in a demanding operational environment through a systematic programme of absence management.

Equally, effective benchmarking can also provide a mechanism for identifying more innovative practices drawn from other business or employment sectors. While for the purposes of statistical comparison it is helpful to begin by benchmarking with broadly similar organisations, it may also be valuable to draw comparisons with substantially different types of operation. For example, it might be that although our absence levels are broadly comparable with other similar organisations', they are still significantly higher than those of organisations in other sectors. If so, it may be illuminating to explore the reasons for this difference. We may conclude that it simply reflects factors that lie outside our control – such as differences in the type of work. More likely, though, we may identify possible solutions which can, with appropriate customisation, be translated into our own industry or occupational sector. Experience suggests, for example, that public-sector organisations can often learn from the commercial disciplines that are generally applied in successful private-sector business. Equally, on the other hand, private-sector businesses can often draw useful lessons from the creativity that is applied in many parts of the public sector to develop relatively low-cost solutions. In gathering and analysing benchmark data, therefore, it is often helpful not merely to focus on obvious comparator organisations (even though these may be the primary source of statistical data) but also to incorporate some more extreme comparators. You might wish, for instance, simply to identify and include the organisations with the best attendance records in your locality, regardless of their characteristics or sector.

Finally, effective benchmarking should ideally be

continuous. You might begin by establishing baseline data to inform your initial planning and prioritisation. From this starting-point, however, you should aim to collect data periodically in order to assess your progress against the comparator group, as well as to gather data on any emerging issues or trends among the group. For example, it may be that overall absence levels are being affected, positively or negatively, by broader national, regional or sectoral factors – the economic environment, changes in legislation or regulation relating to the sector, and so on. By tracking how your own progress matches that of the other comparator organisations, you can assess your own relative success, as well as potentially identifying factors which might be more effectively addressed collectively by the participant organisations. In some cases, indeed, a benchmarking group may take on a much more proactive role, not simply sharing data but working together to develop potential approaches. This might include developing collective responses to common sectoral issues – for example, common health or stress issues that are perceived to affect absence levels – or the testing or piloting of a range of initiatives within individual members of the participating organisations, so that the most successful can then be rolled out to the wider group.

Conclusion

In summary, then, benchmarking is concerned with establishing realistic targets for improvement, as well for informing the potential prioritisation, planning and implementation of potential solutions. Data may be gathered either from the regular national surveys or by participating in initiatives with other organisations. Ideally, the process incorporates a mix of reliable statistical data and qualitative information about respective organisational characteristics and approaches. The benchmark group might include both direct comparator organisations, from within relevant industry sectors, location and organisational types, as well as perhaps some more 'extreme' comparators to help challenge existing thinking or to identify alternative approaches. The results will be both measurable targets for achievement on a department-by-department basis and the generation of qualitative ideas about the content of any new absence-reduction initiatives.

6 ANALYSING THE CAUSES OF ABSENCE

In Chapter 5, we discussed the gathering of information about the current scale and cost of absence in the organisation, and the use of benchmarking to inform targets for achievement. The next step is to analyse in detail the nature of the organisation's absence problem, ensuring that any policy initiatives proposed are appropriate to the causes of the problem and sensitive to the organisation's culture. This is a critical step, but one which is sometimes overlooked in the eagerness to take some practical action. In truth, there is no point in introducing policies to tackle causes of absence that do not exist or grafting on ideas which have worked elsewhere but which may be ineffective in an organisation with a totally different cultural setting. Moreover, if we attempt to introduce inappropriate solutions, we may actually exacerbate the problem by further undermining employee morale.

Beginning to analyse the causes of absence

If we are to ensure a thorough understanding of the causes of absence in the organisation, we must adopt a systematic approach which draws on a mix of quantitative and qualitative data. This can be achieved in a number of ways. The first step is to analyse the absence records to identify the causes of absence that have been provided by employees. However, although this data is essential as a starting-point, we have to recognise that its value and reliability may suffer from some limitations, not least because the formal reasons given for absence may not always accurately reflect the underlying causes. At the most basic level, an employee who is malingering is unlikely to say so! More importantly, though, employees who are suffering from problems of, say, stress or low morale may well ascribe their absence to causes that are perceived as more 'legitimate' to the organisation. Consideration of the formal absence records, therefore, should be treated merely as the start of the analytical process, designed to help identify potential trends, patterns and issues rather than to provide definitive conclusions. Moreover, it is essential that the causes of absence are recorded and categorised in ways that support meaningful analysis of the overall data. Of the two subjects of our case studies, the Scottish Prison Service found it initially necessary to simplify and rationalise the categories against which absence was recorded in order to inform management decision-making and actions.

As a starting-point it is useful to identify the proportion of total absence that can be accounted for by medically certificated longer-term sickness, as distinct from short self-certificated spells. Although both types of absence present organisational difficulties, the nature of the problem and of its likely causes may well be different. A high level of short-term uncertificated absence might be indicative of cultural or attitudinal issues within the organisation, such as poor morale, low job satisfaction, ineffective supervision, and so on. Conversely, high levels of longer-term absence may be more indicative of straightforwardly health-related problems – such as the overall health of the workforce, stress levels, or particular environmental factors. In both cases it is probable that steps can be taken to improve absence levels, but the nature and focus of the interventions are likely to be very different.

Equally, it is important to analyse the patterns of absence, ideally by key variables such as department, occupational group, grade or location. It might be, for example, that absence levels are particularly high at certain times of the year or on specific working patterns. Perhaps there is a high incidence of absences on Mondays or Fridays, either universally or within specific employee groups. Once these types of patterns are identified, you can then begin to relate them to specific organisational factors or characteristics, which in turn may begin to illuminate the potential causes of absence. For example, if absence rises significantly at certain points in the year (other than the predictable increases ascribable to seasonal illnesses), it may be possible to relate this to specific peaks of work activity or similar operational factors. If absence is especially high on particular working patterns, it might be indicative either of a general dissatisfaction with the required working hours or even of more basic considerations such as transport difficulties.

It is also important to find out the extent to which total absence can be accounted for by specific groups of individuals. It is not uncommon to discover that an apparently significant absence problem can, in practice, be largely ascribed to a relatively small number of employees, perhaps within some relatively clearly-defined categories. In such cases there may be little point in investing in a large-scale across-the-board initiative if the problem can be largely resolved by some focused interventions with specific individuals or groups.

Gathering qualitative data

A statistical analysis of absence patterns within the organisation provides essential baseline data for beginning to identify the characteristics and causes of absence. By linking these patterns to broader operational and organisational considerations, we can begin to draw conclusions about the factors that appear to be influencing absence levels across the organisation. However, it is important that we do not jump to conclusions. It is easy to assume, for example, that a high incidence of short-term uncertificated absence must be indicative of malingering and is therefore most appropriately addressed through a punitive approach, such as the withholding of occupational sick pay or the application of disciplinary procedures. That may be an appropriate approach – but the absence levels may additionally or alternatively be indicative of more deep-rooted organisational problems, such as issues of morale, culture or management style. If so, although a punitive approach may bring some short-term improvements, it will probably only exacerbate the problems in the longer term because the underlying causes have not been addressed. Absence levels may begin to rise again, or the dissatisfactions may simply find expression in other ways – declining productivity, increasing staff turnover, and so on.

Having identified any key patterns or trends in the absence data, therefore, we must gather more qualitative data that will help us get behind the bare statistics. It may, for example, be useful to gather the views and opinions of supervisors and line managers. Ideally, where the organisational climate is felt to be appropriate, steps should also be taken to gather the views of employees across the organisation.

In smaller organisations, opinions can be gathered by means of face-to-face interviews or group discussions, whereas in larger organisations a written questionnaire-based survey may be more appropriate. The latter also has the advantage that it can be conducted anonymously and may therefore encourage more frank and honest replies. Careful thought must be given to the contents of interviews or questionnaires to ensure that they explore the causes that are relevant to the circumstances of a given organisation.

The checklist below summarises a range of potential causes of absence drawn from the earlier chapters of the book. In practice, not all will be relevant to every organisation. It is therefore necessary to select those that are most likely to be relevant to particular organisational circumstances. In many cases, the most effective approach will be to use the available statistical data to develop initial hypotheses about the likely nature and causes of absence in the organisation, as described above. The interviews or questionnaire can then be used to test and explore these hypotheses in detail. Alternatively (or additionally), it may be helpful to organise some initial 'focus groups' of managers and employees to discuss the issue of absence. These focus groups do not at this stage need to be statistically representative of the organisation, but they should include an appropriate cross-section of the workforce in terms of variables such as grade, occupation and location. Each group can include a mix of these different variable sets, although it is generally preferable to separate grades or levels of staff so that participants do not feel constrained from speaking openly in front of their managers or subordinates.

Clearly, if the organisation's absence problems appear to be largely concentrated in a particular area, such as a specific function or location, you may wish to restrict the data-gathering to this area. However, even in such cases, it is often helpful to seek the views of a wider group, since this enables you to compare the views expressed in apparent problem areas with those of the wider organisation. This comparison may be revealing in, for example, highlighting differing reactions to apparently similar organisational factors – for instance, one group may be motivated and stimulated by changing organisational requirements whereas another group may perceive such changes as a significant source of stress.

Conducting initial focus groups

These initial focus groups are best conducted in a relatively open, semi-structured format, enabling each group to explore the issues surrounding absence without excessive external direction or leadership. It may be helpful to begin by asking the group to 'brainstorm' the most significant causes of absence in the organisation. The group's unprompted responses to this suggestion will provide a valuable indication of their own sense of priorities in this area. The results of the brainstorming can then be explored in more detail, along with any additional issues that the group facilitator may wish to introduce.

In addition, the facilitator may wish to stimulate discussions by presenting to the group an overview of the absence statistics for the organisation, highlighting any specific areas of interest or concern, such as differences in absence levels between different parts of the organisation. The group can then explore these specific issues, providing their views on the reasons for the variations in absence levels. This can often be a useful means of examining or challenging statements from the group that might appear glib or partial. For example, if the group's initial reaction is to blame work demands for causing stress-related absence, it may be fruitful to ask the group to review absence levels in areas where work requirements are very different. This may help to confirm their view, or it may raise further questions, encouraging the group to acknowledge a wider range of causal factors.

Overall, the aim should be to encourage the group to talk

openly and frankly, rather than simply to express the accepted 'party line' within the organisation. In a high-pressure business, for example, managers may be reluctant to acknowledge problems with stress, which might be perceived as expressions of weakness or inability to cope. Similarly, managers may be tempted to allocate the 'blame' for absence primarily on their subordinates, rather than acknowledging broader problems of management style or culture. Equally, non-management employees may prefer to ascribe absence problems primarily to problems with management, rather than acknowledging cultural or attitudinal problems at more junior levels in the organisation.

Nevertheless, if skilfully facilitated, the dynamic of a group discussion will generally enable participants gradually to address issues more openly, particularly if a diverse range of opinion is being expressed. Furthermore, by comparing the views of different groups of management and non-management staff, we can begin to develop a more three-dimensional view of the organisation, highlighting recurrent themes as well as differences in perceptions. This in turn will provide guidance on the issues to be tested or explored further in subsequent groups or in the survey itself.

Validating the conclusions: a questionnaire

In a smaller organisation it may be sufficient to conduct a programme of focus groups and interviews. In a larger organisation it is generally helpful to validate this information through a questionnaire-based survey, either on a stand-alone basis or as part of a broader employee opinion survey. Ideally, it is preferable to conduct the survey on an anonymous basis, so that respondents are encouraged to express their views fully and openly. However, it is essential that the questionnaire includes at least basic demographic data to enable the responses to be analysed meaningfully. This might, for example, include department location, job-type and grade-level. In practice, there is always a need to balance the desire for anonymity with the need to collect meaningful demographic data – if the latter is too detailed, participants may perceive a risk that they can be identified. Care should be taken, therefore, to collect only demographic data that will genuinely be used to inform subsequent analysis, and to explain very clearly to participants why this data is needed and how it will be used.

The detail of the questionnaire can be developed in a variety of ways, depending on the level and complexity of the information required. As a minimum, the questionnaire should enable you to assess the strength of response to the potential causes of absence identified. In its simplest form, the questionnaire might simply present a list of potential causes, distilled from the focus group responses, and ask respondents to rate each of the possible causes on a scale from, say, '1' (highly insignificant cause) to '6' (highly significant cause) for each employee category. An even number of ratings avoids a middle rating which does not produce useful information, and forces respondents to rate causes as either significant or not. Such an approach will produce a rank order of causes, as these are perceived to relate to different categories of staff. This in turn can be analysed by the various respondent groups, highlighting any significant trends or variations in perception.

If required, more sophisticated survey tools can be applied to explore these issues in more detail. For example, it is possible to design question frameworks which will 'drill' down into specific topic areas, enabling the survey to gather relatively precise information about employee perceptions, preferences or priorities. If, for example, stress is perceived to be a significant cause, it may be appropriate to gather more information about the nature and levels of stress that are perceived by employees. For example, respondents might be asked to rate a range of potential 'stressors' in terms of their perceived impact on absence levels, and to provide guidance on the steps that would be most likely to reduce organisational stress and improve attendance. Similarly, if the focus group findings indicate that the organisation's prevailing management style may be influencing absence levels, the questionnaire might seek respondents' views about the nature and quality of management in the organisation, about their own line managers, or about the kinds of changes that would improve management effectiveness.

At a more pragmatic level, if the focus groups indicate that absence levels are being adversely affected by factors such as unsocial working patterns, domestic difficulties or transport problems, the questionnaire can be used to gather detailed information about specific requirements or preferences. For example, it is not uncommon to find that relatively small changes in working patterns can bring significant benefits in terms of domestic convenience – by providing easier access to public transport, childcare, and so on. Similarly, it might be that absence levels can be significantly reduced by providing greater flexibility in responding to external or domestic factors. In many organisations, for instance, it is in practice more 'legitimate' to be absent (as this can be justified on grounds of illness, even though the absence is uncertificated) than to be late. If employees are facing domestic difficulties, such as problems with childcare, which are going to cause them to arrive late, they may well prefer to call in as 'sick'. In such cases, the availability of some form of 'emergency leave', which can be taken at short notice within defined limits (perhaps repayable through subsequent unpaid overtime), can often have a positive impact on overall absence levels. An effectively designed questionnaire can help the organisation to identify the precise types of provision most likely to meet employees' specific needs.

In the checklist below, we have enumerated some of the most commonly-cited causes of absence within organisations. In each case, we have then highlighted some of the issues and questions that might be explored in both focus groups and written questionnaires in order to gather more information. Depending on the outcomes of the initial focus groups, it would be possible to construct an appropriate validation questionnaire by selecting the relevant items from the list and, using the outline questions provided, construct a detailed questionnaire that would provide reliable and meaningful data in the required areas. However, it should be stressed that considerable care is needed in both the design and application of written employee questionnaires.

First, it is important not to be over-ambitious in the size and scope of the questionnaire. In practice, if the questionnaire is intended to provide detailed information on the selected issues, it will probably be inappropriate to focus on more than four or five key themes. If you attempt to gather data on all the potential causes of absence, you are likely to produce a highly unwieldy questionnaire, which will be confusing for respondents and difficult to interpret meaningfully. You will therefore have to prioritise carefully the topics to be addressed, identifying those factors that you believe likely to have the most significant impact on absence levels in the organisation. At the same time it is a good idea also to underpin the questionnaire with a more general question asking respondents to rate the importance of potential causes to ensure that your initial assumptions are correct.

Second, you should ensure that the questionnaire provides appropriately detailed and meaningful data to inform subsequent decision-making and action in the areas concerned. One of the most common shortcomings of employee surveys is that they tend only to provide a relatively superficial perspective on the issues addressed, highlighting apparent problems without providing sufficient information to inform potential solutions. This is a particular problem of the familiar survey format in which respondents are asked to indicate their level of agreement or disagreement with a series of statements. Although this format can be a useful means of exploring employee attitudes to a range of topics, without careful design it can severely constrain the information gathered. The survey may, for instance, indicate that respondents have a generally negative attitude to a particular topic, but provide relatively little information on the reasons behind this attitude or the potential steps that might be taken to address it.

For this reason, it is often more helpful to apply a range of question formats – for example, not only exploring respondents' attitudes to specific topics but also seeking their views on the relative importance of possible causes or the relative value of potential solutions. Although a survey cannot in itself provide the solutions to absence problems, a carefully designed questionnaire can directly and meaningfully inform potential responses. Yet it is also true that, in crude terms, the longer and more complex the questionnaire, the lower will be the response rate, with consequences for the quality

and representativeness of the data gathered. It is always necessary to strike a balance – ensuring that the questionnaire
is as short and as simple as is practicable, consistent with
collecting meaningful data in priority areas.

Third, at a more basic level, it is important to ensure that
the questionnaire is clear, unambiguous and easy to complete.
There is always a risk – if the questionnaire is being developed
by managers who have been heavily involved in all aspects
of the absence-management programme – that they may take
for granted a level of knowledge which is not actually shared
by the workforce at large – for example, about HR termin-
ology, details of working patterns, arrangements for sick pay,
and so on. Equally, the questionnaire may prove to be too
long, confusing to complete, or unclear or ambiguous in its
content. If the questionnaire refers to 'management' or 'managers', for instance, it may be necessary to define clearly the
level of management in question. If the questionnaire has not
been used previously, it is always worth conducting a limited
pilot among a suitable cross-section of staff, seeking feedback
on both the content and the ease of completion.

Consultation and ownership

Most importantly, it is essential that the survey is not
launched until consideration has been given to the entire
absence-control programme discussed in this section and
there is clear top-management commitment to carry out this
exploratory research. The conducting of any employee survey
can potentially have a significant impact on the organisation,
regardless of its purpose and findings. It may raise difficult
issues that will have to be addressed – for example, about
management style or culture. It may be perceived as threat-
ening both by managers and by the workforce at large, who
may see the content as implicitly critical of their own performance within the organisation. It may well provide
expression for concerns or criticisms that have previously
been suppressed, and that will then have to be managed and
resolved. Above all, it will raise expectations that some form
of action will be taken to address the issues that have been
raised. All too often, surveys are seen as an end in themselves,

an academic data-gathering exercise, which does not lead to any subsequent response or action. This is not only a waste of the organisation's time and resources, it is also likely to leave respondents feeling even more disaffected.

It is critical, therefore, that the purpose and proposed outcomes of the research are clear from the outset, and that there is full commitment to these from all key stakeholders in the organisation. In Chapter 7 we examine the practical steps needed to plan, develop and implement a comprehensive and effective absence-management programme, including processes for ensuring effective consultation and involvement from both senior and operational management across the organisation. It is essential that there is similar consultation and ownership during this exploratory research. Otherwise, there is a risk not only of reducing the value of the research but also of undermining the credibility of the overall absence-management initiative. If, for example, managers feel threatened by the content of the exploratory survey, they are likely to be critical of the overall process.

It is worth bearing in mind that while in theory all parties should be in favour of reducing absence levels, in practice both managers and staff may resent the implied criticism of their current performance in this area (in terms either of their own attendance or of their management of others'). At the start of the exploratory phase, therefore, it is important to establish appropriate mechanisms to involve stakeholders from across the organisation. This might include, for example:

☐   appropriate presentations to the senior management team and any other relevant bodies, such as trade unions or staff associations, setting out the absence issues and costs, the background and content of the proposed research, the level and type of support that will be required of stakeholders, and an indication of how the research findings will be used

☐   consultation with key operational managers – for example, those with large numbers of operational staff or who are currently experiencing significant absence problems: it will be important to stress that the process is intended as supportive and constructive, designed to provide operational managers with the tools and techniques to manage absence effectively, rather than as a criticism of current performance

☐ the establishment of a steering group to oversee the design and implementation of the required interviews and survey – it is often helpful to establish a small but broadly representative cross-functional group to provide input into the process: this ensures both that the activity is appropriately 'owned' by line management (rather than being perceived as an HR imposition) and that there is effective consultation about the content, focus and priorities of the research.

In practice, consultation about the research can be aligned with the broader consultation required to support the absence-management programme as a whole (discussed in more detail in Chapter 7). However, it is important that this consultation begins at the earliest possible stage rather than merely at the point where you are beginning to develop or implement the absence-management programme itself. If key stakeholders have been involved in the gathering of data and in the analysis and interpretation of current absence issues, they are much more likely to be committed to the proposals which result.

Identifying potential causes of absence: the checklist

The following causes of absence, together with their implications for absence control, have been identified in this book. The list is not intended to be exhaustive, for there may well be factors specific to particular organisations or types of operation, but it should provide a relatively comprehensive summary of the key issues to be considered when investigating the dynamics and causality of absence. Clearly, each of these factors must be considered in the light of available statistical data relating to the organisation, and of any initial qualitative data gathered from managers or employees. For example, it is evident that the personal characteristics of employees may have a significant impact on individual and collective absence levels. It may be helpful, therefore, to

Personal characteristics of employees	Issue/Trends	Possible solutions	Issues and questions for investigation
Length of service	Absence levels tend to be higher where length of service is shorter.	Introduction of initiatives or actions to reduce labour turnover.	• What is the organisation's overall profile in terms of length of service? • Is staff turnover higher in specific work-groups? • What are the dynamics/causes of staff turnover?
Age	Older employees tend to suffer more sickness absence.	Improved health screening at recruitment or on a continuing basis for older staff. Introduction of occupational health programmes.	• What is the age-profile of the workforce? • What are actual absence patterns among particular age-groups? • In practice, what are the major causes of sickness absence, and what practical steps can be taken to address them?
Gender	Younger females tend to have higher absence than males of equivalent ages. However, consideration must be given to the potential influence of domestic or family responsibilities as an underlying cause.	Introduction of childcare support, more flexible working patterns or other forms of family-friendly employment policies.	• What is the gender-profile of the workforce? • What is the gender-profile of specific work-groups? Is there a significantly higher percentage of women or men in particular parts of the organisation? • In practice, what factors influence absence levels for each gender? What practical steps might be taken to address them?
Education and career opportunities	Higher educational qualifications and opportunities to pursue a career tend to result in lower absence levels.	The provision of education and training at the workplace, together with policies for internal promotion and opportunities to learn new skills.	• What is the educational profile of the workforce? • Does the educational profile differ significantly between different work-groups? • What kinds of career aspirations do employees have? • What practical steps could be taken to improve career or progression opportunities?

Past absence patterns	Past absence patterns for individual employees have been shown to be useful indicators of future absence.	Improved screening at recruitment and selection, including more effective use of references, and pre-employment health questionnaires and medicals.	• What data is currently available on past absence patterns? • What practical steps could be taken to improve the availability and quality of this data?
Family size	Absence has been found to be linked to family size, although again this may commonly be linked to issues of childcare and other domestic responsibilities.	Again, the introduction of childcare support, more flexible working patterns or other forms of family-friendly employment policies.	• In practice, what domestic or family-related factors are influencing individual absence levels? • What practical steps can be taken to address these?
Employee attitudes, values, work orientations and commitment	Negative employee attitudes and low commitment to the organisation or work activities are associated with higher absence levels. These may be closely linked to the job and organisational factors referred to below.	Improved assessment processes at recruitment and selection to ensure most appropriate match of individual to the organisation/role. Potential initiatives to enhance commitment through employee communication, participation, involvement, job redesign and teamworking.	• What is the overall culture of the workforce? Does this differ significantly between different work-groups? • What are the factors that influence culture and attitudes within the organisation? • What practical steps can be taken to address these factors?

Job and organisational factors	Issue/Trends	Possible solutions	Issues and questions for investigation
Work design	Absence is commonly related to lack of job satisfaction arising from routine and boring work.	Initiatives to redesign or reallocate work activities, perhaps through job enrichment or rotation. Teamworking initiatives which provide greater autonomy for work-groups in controlling their work activities.	• How do absence levels differ between work groups? Do they appear to be linked to variations in the type or level of the work? • What are employees' perceptions of their work activities? In practice, does this affect their absence levels? • What practical steps can be taken to improve work activities?
Stress	Work-related stress is increasingly being recognised as a significant cause of absence. In practice, stress may result from a variety of underlying causes, and these must be assessed in detail. Potential causes include poor or unsafe working conditions, boredom, work overload, perceived lack of control over work activities, job insecurity, worry over career and promotional prospects, and workplace relationships. In addition, stress may arise from sources outside the workplace.	Depending on the nature and causes of stress in the workplace, initiatives might include occupational health activities, employee assistance programmes, and individual counselling. Stress might also be reduced through organisational changes in areas such as work design, management style, communications and resourcing.	• What levels and types of stress are evident in the organisation? Do these vary significantly between different work-groups? To what extent do these appear to be affecting absence levels? • What appear to be the major causes of stress in the organisation? • What is the mix of individual, organisational and external factors? • What practical steps can be taken to address these factors? (Note: although questions on stress may be built into a general investigatory survey, there are a number of well-validated stress audit tools available which enable the organisation to benchmark its stress levels against external norms.)
Organisation and work-group size	Absence levels tend to be higher the larger the organisation and the larger the size of the work-group.	Possible de-layering or subdividing of organisations into smaller business units or profit centres, or establishing smaller, team-based work-groups. This may be particularly appropriate in larger, more impersonal organisational units, such as telephone contact centres.	• Do absence levels appear to vary according to the size of the work-group? • If so, what factors are influencing absence levels – eg nature of the work, management style, belief that individual absence does not affect colleagues, etc? • What practical steps can be taken to address these factors?

Work-group norms and cultures	Such norms and cultures are often embedded in the history and traditions of an organisation, reflecting the priority given by management to absence control, and past willingness and ability to enforce sanctions. Where high absence control has been given a low priority, absence levels are likely to be high. Where management has laid out clear rules of conduct and enforced them consistently and fairly, absence levels are likely to be lower. Peer-group pressure is also often a significant factor in enforcing high standards of attendance.	Initiatives to devolve decision-making, empowering teams to increased control of and accountability for their own activities and performance, so requiring the team to take greater collective responsibility for attendance. Arrangements such as pre-paid committed overtime, on-call rotas, banked contingency time and annualised hours can also increase employees' awareness of the negative impact of their colleagues' absence.	• What has been the history of absence management in the organisation? Have high levels of absence traditionally been tolerated, either in the organisation as a whole or in particular work-groups? Have rules and procedures been applied clearly and consistently? • What attitudes do employees have to absence? Do they perceive current absence levels as reasonable and acceptable? Do they perceive some managers or work-groups as more tolerant of absence than others? What do they believe are the real causes of absence in the organisation? What impact do they believe absence has on their own workload? • What practical steps can be taken to address these perceptions?
Sick-pay policies	Relationships have been found between the establishment of occupational sick-pay schemes and higher absence, so that time off is seen almost as an 'entitlement'. Needless to say, we would not advocate the withdrawal of occupational sick-pay schemes, but aspects of their operation may need consideration.	Potential amendments to the detail or operation of the occupational sick-pay scheme – eg making payments subject to management's discretion, with the opportunity to withhold payment where there is clear evidence of abuse. Other options include lengthening the period of service before entitlement commences, not paying for uncertificated absence, or paying for the first few days of absence only after the absence has reached a certain length (although this must be introduced carefully if it is not to 'encourage' staff to take longer periods of absence so they reach the threshhold).	• What is the actual pattern of absence in the organisation? For example, is there a high incidence of short-term uncertificated absence, either generally or in specific work-groups? • Again, what are employees' attitudes to absence? Do they believe that the availability of sick pay 'legitimises' absence? Do they believe that some employees tend to abuse this entitlement? • What would be the perceived impact of increased constraints on the availability of sick pay?

External factors	Issue/Trends	Possible solutions	Issues and questions for investigation
Economic and market conditions	Absence tends to rise in times of economic boom and fall in times of recession. During economic upturns, additional job opportunities are available and people are apparently less concerned about losing a job as a result of disciplinary sanctions. During economic downturns, people become more concerned about job security and are less likely to take time off.	Organisations can do little to manage these external economic factors, but they should interpret their absence statistics and trends accordingly. Although some rise in absence may occur in economic upturns, this should not prevent organisations from applying absence-control policies and sanctions to counter them. Equally, it may not be sensible for the organisation to exploit job insecurity to adopt a more punitive approach, because this may simply store up resentment for the future. Ideally, the organisation should interpret its absence trends in the light of prevailing economic conditions, but apply consistent standards and approaches.	• What are employee attitudes to job security and their own employability? What factors influence these perceptions? To what extent do these attitudes affect employees' views of attendance? • What practical steps can be taken to increase employees' intrinsic commitment to the organisation or to their current roles?
Genuine illness	It has been reckoned that this accounts for between a half and two thirds of all absence and is probably the most significant of all the causes of absence we have considered.	Although it is not appropriate to compel or encourage sick employees to attend work, the nature and causes of illness can of course be highly varied. It is clear, for example, that factors such as stress, personal and emotional problems, smoking and alcohol abuse may be underlying causes of a significant proportion of sickness absence. In practice, much can be done to tackle these issues, including pre-employment health questionnaires and medicals, policies on smoking at work and alcohol abuse, the promotion of better health awareness, programmes of preventative healthcare (such as flu vaccinations or health checks), employee assistance programmes and counselling.	• What are the stated causes of sickness absence in the organisation? Are any patterns evident, either generally or for particular work groups? • What practical steps can be taken to improve the overall health of the workforce or to address recurrent sickness problems identified?

Family responsibilities	Otherwise highly motivated employees may, from time to time, experience constraints in their ability to attend because of family or domestic responsibilities. These may include the illness of children or other family members, or domestic crises. Managers in the CBI's (1997) survey rated family or domestic responsibilities as the second most significant cause of absence after colds and flu.	As outlined above, a range of policies can be adopted to address issues in this area. Options include flexitime – enabling employees to build up additional leave entitlements by accruing banks of additional hours worked – or emergency leave arrangements. Other potential areas of flexibility include a willingness to allow employees to transfer from full-time to part-time working, to job-share or to work permanently or occasionally from home.	• What do employees perceive as the major causes of 'non-medical' absence? What domestic issues cause problems for employees in meeting their work commitments (even if these are currently handled without necessarily being absent)? • What practical steps would improve employees' ability to handle domestic problems which might otherwise conflict with their work commitments?
Travel difficulties	Absence levels rise the longer the journey to work, when the weather is poor, where road traffic is particularly congested, or where travel options are constrained by location or time of working. These factors serve to create constraints on people's abilities to attend even if in normal circumstances they are motivated to do so.	Screening at recruitment might usefully explore the nature of the journey a prospective employee will have to make. Provisions such as company transport services or the co-ordination of car pooling may be appropriate, especially if the workplace or some working patterns are poorly served by public transport. Other options include greater flexibility to work remotely where transport is problematic.	• What is the organisation's 'travel to work' area? Is there evidence that employees who live more remotely have greater absence problems? Is there evidence of links between absence and factors such as poor weather or other transport problems? • How do employees perceive transport issues? What kinds of problems do they encounter, and what impact do these have on their attendance? • What practical steps could be taken to address the issues identified?

review the various personal characteristics summarised below against the overall demographics of the workforce – what is the profile in terms of, for example, length of service, age, gender, etc? If specific work groups or the workforce as a whole display particular characteristics, such as a relatively high incidence of recent recruits, this may help to indicate a potential cause that can be investigated further.

Under each of the table headings on pages 164–169, we have indicated:

- ☐ the typical trends indicated by existing research and statistics in this field
- ☐ the possible implications for absence management policies and solutions
- ☐ potential issues or questions for further investigation during employee interviews, focus groups or surveys.

The above listing is intended to provide an initial checklist of the major potential causes of absence in the organisation, and a summary of some of the possible steps that may be taken to address these causes. As the list indicates – and as we have stressed throughout this book – the potential causes of absence are many and varied, and it is likely that any organisation (and any work-group within each organisation) will display some combination of the factors set out above. The first step, therefore, is to identify, as precisely as possible, the particular mixture and balance of factors that has the most significant influence on absence within your organisation. By analysing your absence statistics, by reviewing the profile of your workforce against the various dimensions set out above, and by gathering qualitative data about employees' opinions and attitudes, you can begin to establish a reliable picture of the dynamics of absence in your organisation.

On this basis, you can then begin to develop a coherent approach to address those specific factors that are most likely to improve attendance in your organisation. Again, as the list above makes clear, any effective approach to absence management is likely to be multi-dimensional. It may have to address issues of absence policy, culture, management style, domestic issues and constraints, organisation and job design, working patterns, pay and reward, stress management, and numerous other possible considerations. It will not of course be possible (or indeed desirable) to address all these areas at the same time. You will therefore have to ensure that your time and resources are invested most productively in the mix of solutions that is likely to have the most significant impact on absence levels, while also ensuring that the resulting initiatives are consistent and, as far as possible, mutually reinforcing. In the final chapter, therefore, we consider in detail the practical steps that must be taken in introducing and operating an effective absence-management programme.

7 IMPLEMENTING AN ABSENCE-MANAGEMENT SYSTEM

In Chapter 6, we described the steps needed to begin analysing the nature, scale and causes of absence within the organisation. In this concluding chapter we explore how, in practical terms, this information can be applied to establish an effective and cost-efficient process for managing absence within your organisation. This chapter will provide both a summary of the key issues and principles outlined in the earlier chapters, and a step-by-step guide to the practicalities of introducing and operating effective absence management.

As we concluded in the previous chapter, the possible causes of absence can be highly varied, relating to a range of individual, organisational and external factors. An effective absence-management programme must therefore be carefully tailored to address the particular factors that are affecting your organisation. Indeed, it may also be necessary to tailor specific aspects of the programme to suit the requirements of particular departments, locations or other work-groups. If you apply a 'one-size-fits-all' approach to a highly heterogeneous or dispersed organisation, you may well find that in many areas substantial resource is being wasted on addressing non-existent problems.

Nevertheless, although customisation may well be required in the detail and application of the programme, effective absence management is still based on a bedrock of core principles and disciplines which need to be applied consistently across the organisation. If this basic foundation is not firmly established and accepted at the start, it is likely that you will encounter continuing difficulties in the practicalities of managing absence at the individual level. We should begin, therefore, by considering the key principles that must be in place across the organisation, and the practical steps to be applied to ensure that these are fully accepted and owned by senior and operational management.

Absence policies and procedures

Regardless of the nature and causes of absence in your organisation, the first step is to ensure that you have in place a clear, consistent and commonly accepted framework for the management of absence. If the organisation lacks transparent policies and procedures in this area, it will always prove difficult to manage absence fairly and rigorously at either the collective or the individual level. Although this is an obvious point, in practice it is still not uncommon to find that absence polices are non-existent or incomplete. Even where appropriate policies exist, they are often documented only in a relatively inaccessible form, such as a central HR manual, with little effective dissemination of their provisions or requirements among operational management.

An effective absence-management policy should encompass the following key elements:

☐ a clear statement of the standards of attendance required by the organisation

☐ full management commitment to the organisation's absence policies and standards

☐ systematic procedures for managing general absence

☐ systematic procedures for investigating and managing 'problem' absence

☐ investigating the background

☐ absence counselling

☐ taking action.

A statement of attendance standards required by the organisation

As we indicated in Chapter 4, one of the common difficulties faced by employees is that there is no consistent definition of the organisation's requirements and expectations in respect of attendance. In such cases, the only guideline is the custom and practice that has become established, which in any case may well vary from manager to manager, or from time to time. Without such boundaries, some employees will inevitably continue to challenge the limits of the organisation's tolerance, while managers may feel unable to address the problem until it becomes relatively extreme. All too often, this results in recurrent pendulum swings, where excessive tolerance is succeeded by sudden clampdowns, leaving employees feeling unfairly treated and the organisation vulnerable to grievances or even, in more extreme cases, employment tribunals.

The starting-point, therefore, should be a definition of the levels of absence that are acceptable within the organisation, and of the types of action that will be taken at particular points. The definition must be carefully structured and phrased to ensure that it does not appear to 'legitimise' limited absence to the point where employees may see this as an entitlement. (We have all heard anecdotes about employees who appear to regard uncertificated absence as an extension of annual paid leave!). Equally, the definition should not unfairly victimise those who are compelled to be absent for legitimate reasons. An effective definition would therefore comprise the following elements:

☐ *the organisational policy on attendance and absence* – an initial statement that employees are paid to attend work during specified hours, and that they are expected to meet their commitments in this respect except where they have genuine and legitimate reasons to be absent. It should be stressed that regardless of the reason, any absence causes the organisation operational difficulties, reduces efficiency, increases costs, requires additional cover, undermines quality or customer service, and so on. At the same time the organisation should confirm its intention to provide all reasonable support and assistance for those who are absent for legitimate reasons, with the aim of facilitating their return to work at the earliest appropriate opportunity. These underlying considerations provide the context for the organisation's overall policies and procedures for absence management. In one of the case studies at the back of this book, James Cropper plc gives an example of a clear statement of the organisation's attitude towards absence.

☐ *absence procedures* – a definition of the basic procedures to be followed by staff who are forced to be absent from work. This will include, for example, requirements for notifying their manager of their expected absence (typically within a defined period following their normal starting-time on the first day of absence), for continuing to update management on the expected length of absence, for the production of medical certificates, and for the procedures to be followed on the individual's return to work. It should be stressed that these requirements are essential, and that any failure to follow them may result in disciplinary action. It may also be worth stressing that responsibility for notification at each stage rests with the employee, and that line managers should not be expected to 'chase up' information regarding absent employees.

☐ *'trigger-points' for extended absence* – the trigger-points that will apply to particular types or lengths of absence, and the actions instigated by those trigger-points at these stages. In practice, two parallel forms of 'trigger points' may be applied. These will include, for example, the point at which medical certificates are required; the stages at which the organisation will contact the individual by telephone, institute a home visit or seek a formal prognosis from its occupational health advisor and/or the individual's GP; the stages at which occupational sick pay would be reduced or discontinued; and so on.

☐ *'trigger-points' for recurrent short-term absence* – the points at which action will be taken in response to recurrent short-term absence – notably, the stage at which the employee might be interviewed by the line manager and/ or HR, as a preliminary to considering more formal action. If the organisation uses the 'Bradford formula' (described in Chapter 1) or some similar indicator, it will be necessary to specify the 'score' that would trigger a formal intervention. First, it is necessary to specify the actions that will be taken at defined points during an extended single period of absence. In the Scottish Prison Service case study, for example (pages 210–215), the triggers were defined as three periods of absence, nine days of sick absence in any rolling period of 12 months, or any discernible pattern of absence that gave cause for concern. It should be stressed that although such trigger-points are intended to provide clear guidelines on the handling of recurrent absence, in practice the organisation will treat each individual case on its merits. So if there is good reason to believe that a specific instance of absence is not legitimate, the organisation may institute investigatory or even disciplinary action immediately, regardless of the individual's previous absence record. Conversely, if the reasons for recurrent absence are legitimate and are known to be temporary (for example, an individual with a problematic but short-term medical condition), it may be appropriate to defer any action until the specific issue is resolved.

Example of an absence policy

Employees in the XYZ Company are paid on the basis of satisfactory attendance and performance. While it is recognised that most employees will occasionally have genuine and acceptable reasons to be absent from work, any absence will cause operational difficulties, undermine our quality and efficiency, and increase our costs. Overall, absenteeism can have a substantial impact on Company profitability and productivity. The aim of this absence policy is therefore to minimise absence levels across the Company, while also providing reasonable support for those absent for legitimate reasons with the aim of assisting their return to work at the earliest opportunity. The policy also aims to ensure that all employees are treated fairly and consistently.

To this end, the Company aims to ensure that:

All policies, rules and procedures concerning absence are communicated clearly to all employees.

Managers and team leaders will apply the procedures fairly and consistently.

The HR function will maintain computer records, based on information received from line managers, indicating the duration and stated reasons for all periods of absence. This information will be used to monitor absence levels, and to indicate where further action may be needed.

Managers and team leaders will interview all employees on their return from absence, regardless of its duration. The purpose of the interview will be to explore the causes of the absence, to facilitate the individual's return to work, and to identify any reasonable and practical steps to reduce the likelihood of future absence.

The HR function will provide support for managers and team leaders in ensuring consistency in dealing with absence and any related issues and, where appropriate, in advising on how individual absence issues should be handled.

Where absence levels exceed specified 'trigger' levels, managers or team leaders are required to take formal action. This includes the conducting of formal absence interviews and the issuing of formal warnings, as set out in the Company's absence management procedures. In extreme cases, excessive absence may result in termination of employment on the grounds of insufficient capability. However, the Company's first priority will always be to achieve satisfactory levels of attendance.

Where an employee is absent on extended sick leave, managers or HR will contact the individual on a regular basis, including conducting periodic home visits, with the aim of facilitating the individual's return to work at the earliest reasonable point.

Where appropriate, the Company may seek advice or guidance from its occupational health advisers in medical issues relating to individual absence.

The Company is committed to supporting the health of its workforce, and provides a range of positive healthcare and fitness initiatives available to all employees.

In dealing with individual absence issues, the Company will aim to act reasonably at all times, taking account of all the circumstances.

Management commitment to the absence policies and standards

The statement of absence policy should therefore provide a clear and unequivocal definition of the organisation's attitudes and expectations regarding absence, and of the responsibilities facing employees in respect of their attendance at work. If the statement is to provide a credible basis for the management of absence, however, it is critical that managers across the whole organisation apply its principles and provisions consistently and rigorously. If employees perceive any inconsistency in application, or if they believe that managers are not fully committed to the standards set out in the statement, the effectiveness of absence management will be rapidly undermined.

As a starting-point, therefore, it is essential to ensure that all managers are fully committed to the organisation's declared standards and provisions for managing absence. If the standards are perceived as unrealistic, or if the absence management process is seen merely as an imposition from the human resource function, the rules are unlikely to be applied effectively. It is worth bearing in mind that whereas managers are on principle usually in favour of effective absence management, in practice they often feel uncomfortable tackling individual absence problems amongst their own teams. It is not easy to question or challenge individual absence levels, particularly if there is genuine doubt over whether the absence is legitimate. In one large organisation which appeared to operate a highly rigorous absence management system, an evaluation study revealed that in nearly three quarters of cases managers had not applied the specified provisions, citing 'exceptional circumstances'!

The first step is to ensure that there is full commitment from the senior levels in the organisation – that is, the board, the senior management team or equivalent. As we indicated in the preceding two chapters, any credible absence management policy has to be underpinned by clear and reliable data on the nature and level of the absence problems facing the organisation, the direct and indirect costs of current absence and its impact on organisational performance, and the steps necessary to address the problems. There should be a clear demonstration that the projected benefits of reducing absence will more than offset the required investment of management time and other resources. Above all – because it will always be difficult to predict the precise impact of any absence-management policy in advance – there should be clearly-defined criteria for evaluating the effectiveness of the process over time. These will include setting targets for reducing absence levels, with a definition of the cost-benefits of the targeted reductions (for example, a 1 per cent reduction in absence will produce £ × savings).

Ideally, we would recommend that this business case is made explicitly to the senior team (the board), along with a clear statement of the level of support and commitment that will be required of operational managers across the business. This provides the senior team with the opportunity to declare its public backing for the policy and the supporting management processes, positioning absence management as a business imperative rather than simply a human resources priority.

Once the senior team has declared its formal 'sponsorship' of the absence-management policy, it will then be possible to seek more active support from operational management in the development and implementation of the required processes. Again, it is critical that there is maximum involvement of operational management. If you are developing new absence-management processes or substantially revising existing procedures, we would recommend establishing a cross-organisational steering group to oversee the project. This should include representation from operational management in all key functions or areas of activity, particularly those employing large numbers of staff, as well as appropriate representation from the HR function.

The role of the steering group is to ensure that the absence policies, standards and procedures genuinely meet the needs of the organisation and can be applied effectively in the operational environment. Ideally, therefore, the group should comprise team leaders and managers who actually have to deal with the realities of absence management on a day-to-day basis within their own areas. It is this group who will have to live with the practicalities of any policies and procedures that are introduced, and who will be best placed to advise whether theoretical good practice is likely to work effectively on the ground. In addition, if the culture of the organisation allows, we would also recommend that the steering group includes representation from trade unions or other representative groups. As we noted in Chapter 3, the majority of trade unions support the principle of effective absence management but often express concern about how the issue is handled in practice, particularly if they believe that management is adopting an unduly punitive approach. If the trade unions can be involved in the development of the policies and practices, they can be reassured about the aims and content of the proposed approach.

The group should review the data and statistics gathered about the nature, levels and causes of absence (as described in Chapters 5 and 6), as the basis for developing appropriate standards, policies and procedures. Key matters for the group to consider might include:

☐ *the existing absence management culture in the organisation* – If, for example, the absence-management culture has formerly been relatively tolerant of high absence levels, the group will have to assess the potential impact of moving towards much more stringent standards. It might be that the immediate application of more stringent standards would bring a positive impact. However, it is perhaps more likely that a dramatic tightening of standards would simply not be perceived as credible, or would not be effectively enforced by managers. In the latter case, it might be more appropriate to adopt an incremental approach, increasing standards over an extended period.

☐ *the existing skill and confidence levels of team leaders and managers in handling absence problems* – As we indicated above, the management of individual absence is often challenging, and managers may be tempted to 'sweep the problem under the carpet' even at the cost of some operational inconvenience or ill-feeling. There is little point in developing rigorous standards at the organisational level if in practice they are ignored by individual managers or team leaders on the shop floor. In reviewing the data on the nature and causes of absence, therefore, it is important also to review the apparent skill and confidence levels of managers in this area. If there is evidence that managers are currently tending to ignore problems, then any tightening of absence-management standards or policies will have to be reinforced by increased support and training for the managers involved. Both of our case study organisations featured at the back of this book, the Scottish Prison Service and James Cropper plc, stressed that systematic training for managers had been a key component in their absence-management strategies.

☐ *operational practicalities* – In developing procedures for managing absence, much will depend on the nature of the organisation's activities, and the specific requirements for attendance in particular areas or functions. If, for example, the organisation carries out activities where resourcing levels are critical, such as production lines, contact centres, and so on, it will generally be appropriate to apply very stringent procedures for reporting and managing absence – for example, requiring employees to report expected absence if possible prior to the start of their scheduled start-time, or providing continuing updates of their expected return dates. This will enable resource levels to be predicted and, where necessary, cover to be obtained. In a more flexible environment, immediate reporting of absence may be less critical, and the emphasis might instead be on ensuring that the cause and likely duration of the absence is reported by a specified time. If the absence management policies are to have credibility with managers and the workforce, it is essential that they are seen as reinforcing operational needs and priorities.

These are all straightforward points, but they are frequently underestimated in the desire to introduce 'best practice' absence management policies. Too often, polices, procedures and standards are taken 'off the shelf', perhaps borrowed from other employers or from reference sources, and are imposed centrally by the HR function, with no real commitment or ownership from the managers who are required to apply them. The involvement of the steering group should provide a channel for exploring these issues, the group members seeking input from their respective constituencies as appropriate. As policies and procedures are developed, the group can then test and investigate their practicality, as well as provide a channel for communicating the outcomes of the work back to their own areas. The overall aim should be to ensure that the absence-management process is perceived as an operational or business initiative, co-ordinated by HR, which is designed to help managers improve the performance and efficiency of their own areas.

Systematic procedures for managing general absence

We indicated above that the absence-management policy should include definitions of the standards and procedures that should apply in the reporting and management of individual absence. Once these have been developed and agreed by the steering group, you will have to ensure that you have the administrative and management systems in place to guarantee that they can be implemented effectively.

Key elements are likely to include:

- [ ] *a system for reporting absence by the individual to the line manager* – As indicated above, this system should define when and how the initial notification of the absence is to be made, and detail ongoing requirements for notifying the line manager as to the expected duration of the absence, for providing medical certificates, and for reporting on return to work. In addition to defining timescales for the above, the procedures should set out how and to whom information should be provided – for example, whether medical certificates are sent to the line manager.

- [ ] *a system for reporting absence to HR or equivalent for central monitoring and support purposes* – There will in any case be a requirement to report absence to HR for administrative purposes – that is, in relation to statutory sick pay and/or internal occupational sick-pay schemes. However, in most cases, it will also be appropriate for HR to hold central records of individual and collective absence, both to inform absence statistics and to help provide support for managers in the handling of individual cases. The increasing use of HR information systems has tended to facilitate communications between managers and HR in this area, whereas traditionally such contact would have relied on paper or telephone communication, the forwarding of medical certificates, and so on. As we noted in Chapter 5, many HR information systems include absence recording modules which can be updated by line managers or local HR staff, allowing an accurate tracking of data over time.

- [ ] *a system for ensuring the appropriate application of absence-management standards and procedures* – Again, this tends to be facilitated by the use of an HR information system which can highlight key trigger-points or other 'alerts'. These might include, for example, triggers for the provision of medical certificates, for necessary updates on the expected duration of the absence or for a return-to-work interview, as well as highlighting when more formal action may be required by the manager. This kind of system can often provide useful disciplines in prompting actions that might otherwise be overlooked by busy managers. For example, in cases of extended absence the system might periodically highlight the need for new medical certificates or to maintain telephone contact with the individual. Similarly, the system might, alongside the recording of the individual's return to work, require a summary of the outcomes of a return-to-work interview.

☐ *a clear procedure for communicating with staff who are absent* – As we have indicated in preceding chapters, it is essential to maintain effective contact with absent staff, regardless of the nature or 'legitimacy' of their absence. In practice, of course, the form of this contact will vary depending on the characteristics and duration of their absence, but it is essential that contact is made and maintained from the earliest appropriate stage. This demonstrates to the individual that the manager is taking the absence seriously, while also providing the manager with the information needed on a continuing basis to ensure that any appropriate action is being taken. The precise approach may depend on the culture and norms of the organisation – for example, in some organisations there is little or no tradition of contacting employees at their home addresses, and it may therefore take some time to establish this as 'standard' practice. Nevertheless, it will normally be appropriate to communicate on the following basis for extended or recurrent absence:

– In addition to the requirement for an individual to advise on the likely duration of the absence, the manager should initiate telephone contact with the individual after a defined period of absence (say, five working days) and thereafter on a weekly basis. These calls should not normally be investigatory in a formal sense but should simply involve enquiring about the individual's condition and prognosis, and identifying any practical steps that the organisation might take to help the individual. The call should be standard practice in the organisation for all extended absences, and should not be seen as implying any suspicion of the legitimacy of the absence or as placing any unreasonable pressure on the individual to return to work inappropriately. However, this contact will help the manager to decide what subsequent action might be needed, and at what point it might be necessary to institute more formal action or investigation. If, for example, the individual is absent through some clearly-defined injury, there may be no question about the legitimacy of the absence, but it may be appropriate to explore the kind of practical support that might facilitate the individual's return to work. If the causes of the absence are less clearly defined (for example, some form of stress-related illness), the manager may have to decide when to initiate some further investigation through a home visit or via an occupational health adviser.

– When absence is protracted, for whatever reason, it will normally be appropriate to pay a visit to the individual's home, carried out either by the line manager or by a representative of HR. The purposes and benefits of the home visit are severalfold. As with telephone contact, it helps to ensure that the manager has sufficient knowledge of the individual's condition to inform any necessary actions, either to provide any needed support or to initiate further investigation. From the individual's perspective it helps to ensure that a constructive relationship is maintained with the manager and the organisation throughout the period of the absence. This may be particularly valuable in cases of extended absence, where individuals can begin to feel very detached and isolated from their working environment, while perhaps also being concerned about the potential reactions of their manager and colleagues. Although the system should therefore include some form of trigger for this once the individual has been absent for a defined period (say, 15 working days), the precise timing may depend on the nature of the individual's absence. Again, where the reasons for the absence are less clearly defined or understood, it may be appropriate to initiate the visit at an earlier stage in order to ensure that appropriate actions are being taken. Where the reasons for the absence are well understood, it may not be necessary to initiate an early visit, but it may well be useful to conduct a visit at a later stage when the individual is beginning to prepare for a return to work.

☐ *a clear procedure for managing an employee's return to work* – Regardless of the duration of the absence, some form of return-to-work interview should be conducted. (Both of our case study organisations, the Scottish Prison Service and James Cropper plc, emphasised the importance of ensuring rigour and consistency in such interviews.) This is not only a demonstration of the organisation's commitment to managing absence proactively but an opportunity to gather information about the nature and causes of the absence, and any steps that might be taken to reduce the likelihood of future absence. Where the individual has been absent only for a short period, with no history of recurrent absence, the discussion is likely to be relatively short and informal. It would simply review the reasons for the absence and any other information that might be helpful to the manager (for example, the possibility of recurrence or the need for any future treatment). Where there is some history of recurrent absence (even though this may not yet be sufficient to trigger formal investigation or action), it may be appropriate to explore the reasons for the absence in more depth, to see if there are any underlying factors that might be addressed. Finally, where the individual has been absent for an extended period, the interview might focus on the actions needed to facilitate the individual's effective return to work, and any support that might reduce the risk of further absence. For instance, if the individual has suffered from some form of muscular or skeletal injury, it may be appropriate to review the nature of the individual's work activities or environment to reduce the likelihood of repeated or associated injuries.

Systematic procedures for investigating and managing 'problem' absence

Although all absence is potentially problematic from an operational perspective, the absence policy should clearly define the types and levels of absence that are likely to merit more formal investigation and/or action on the part of the organisation. These more formal interventions will normally be triggered by a review of both the total number of days absent and the number of instances of absence in a given period, as we noted in Chapter 3. Again, in practice, many HR information systems now include automatic triggers that can be used to alert the line manager or the relevant HR representative when absence reaches pre-defined levels. Once these trigger-points are reached, in respect of an individual employee, it will normally be necessary for the line manager to initiate some kind of formal action, typically beginning with an investigation of the circumstances surrounding the absence.

As we have indicated in preceding chapters, the key to managing individual absence lies in the application of consistent, rigorous standards and procedures, alongside a thorough understanding of the circumstances of each individual case. In practice, each individual absence record will be different, involving any of various types of absence and a range of potential underlying causes. It is critical that the actions taken by line managers and HR staff fully and appropriately reflect the characteristics of the specific case. If you initiate actions that are inappropriate to the circumstances of the case, you are likely to be treating the employee unreasonably.

It is essential, therefore, that the organisation has in place a systematic procedure to be followed for investigating and reviewing absence issues *prior* to taking any formal management action. Although it is important that ultimate responsibility should lie with the line manager, we would also recommend close consultation between the manager and relevant HR staff, to ensure that appropriate procedures are being followed and that there is consistency of practice across the organisation as a whole.

As always, the extreme cases are relatively easy to deal with. If there is strong evidence that high levels of absence are simply the result of malingering, it will clearly be appropriate to move quickly to formal disciplinary action. Equally, if the absence levels result from genuine and unavoidable health problems, the organisation must consider the practical implications of the condition, identify potential steps that might be applied to alleviate its impact on attendance, and review the likely prognosis of the condition, consulting appropriately with occupational health advisers, the individual's own GP, and so on. Both types of absence of course bring their own significant challenges and problems, but at least the application of formal procedures is likely to be comparatively straightforward.

In reality, however, the majority of absence 'cases' will lie in the grey area between these two extremes, and there will be a continuum of potential characteristics and causes. Towards the 'genuine' end of the spectrum there may be individuals who are experiencing genuine recurrent medical conditions but whose overall attendance record could be significantly improved by, for example, achieving a better general state of health, taking some preventative healthcare action, or perhaps avoiding activities such as intensive sports which lead to minor but recurrent injuries. At the other end of the spectrum there may be employees who are repeatedly unable to attend work because of factors that are relatively controllable – for example, the recurrent Monday-morning hangover following an over-indulgent weekend! In the middle we may encounter employees who are suffering from significant domestic or personal disruptions which affect their attendance, such as carer responsibilities or transport difficulties. Moreover, in practice even these categories will often become blurred. The individual suffering from recurrent hangovers may simply be irresponsible or may be suffering from an alcohol-addiction problem that ought to be treated as a medical condition. The employee with carer responsibilities may also be suffering from high levels of stress, so that it is not possible to draw a clear line between domestic needs and medical incapacity.

Investigating the background

Each of these cases requires different treatment, and the line manager must start by gathering as much information as possible about the nature and causes of the absence. Once the trigger-point has been reached, the first step is normally for the manager to review the statistical and other data relating to possible absence patterns. Key questions might include:

- ☐ Is there any discernible pattern to the absence – eg frequent Monday or Friday absences?
- ☐ What proportion of the absence is certificated or uncertificated?
- ☐ What reasons have been given for previous absence? Are the causes varied or does there appear to be a link between the various absences?
- ☐ What information has been gathered from previous return-to-work interviews?
- ☐ What anecdotal or other evidence might be available about possible underlying causes of absence?

It is important that the manager does not jump to conclusions simply on the basis of this data – particularly in view of the fact that anecdotal or similar information may be highly unreliable – but this kind of analysis will help the manager to identify potential issues to explore with the employee in question.

Absence counselling

The next step is to conduct an absence counselling session with the individual. The style and content of the counselling session was discussed in some detail in Chapter 3, where we noted that although this session is likely to be longer and more wide-ranging than a standard return-to-work interview, it should not at this stage be presented or perceived as part of the disciplinary process. The purpose and style of the meeting should here be a positive and constructive one. The employee should be helped and encouraged to understand that his or her absence levels present a problem to the organisation, and the discussion should then explore the reasons for the absence with the aim of identifying practical steps that might be taken to reduce absence levels in future.

Effective absence counselling requires some skill on the part of the line manager. Indeed, for managers who are dealing with significant numbers of employees, it may well be appropriate as part of the absence-management process for the organisation to provide some training in the skills of absence counselling. Such training would help managers to understand some of the potential causes of absence, the kinds of symptoms that might be indicative of particular causal factors, and the potential approaches to be adopted in reviewing absence issues with employees.

Ideally, the manager – while always reiterating the organisation's declared attendance standards – will aim to establish a spirit of openness and frankness in the discussion, encouraging the employee to discuss as openly as possible any factors that might be affecting his or her attendance. The tactics adopted by the manager may depend on the hypotheses that have been developed on the basis of the existing evidence. For example, the manager may suspect that previous absences have been caused by domestic or similar factors rather than by genuine illness. In such cases it might be appropriate to open the session by 'declaring an amnesty' on previous incidents so that the employee is encouraged to speak openly about the reasons for past absence without any fear of resulting disciplinary action. If, on the other hand, the manager suspects that there may be some underlying medical cause behind a series of supposedly disconnected absences, it may be appropriate to focus supportively on the provision of medical help or advice.

Nevertheless, as we indicated above, experience suggests that the reasons for high absence levels are often multifaceted and complex, and that they may not even be fully understood by the individuals involved. The employee may, for example, be unaware that he or she has some underlying medical condition, or that there may be a underpinning factor such as alcohol dependence, depression or stress which is affecting his or her attendance at work. Even if the employee is aware of these possibilities, the sensitivity of the issues involved may well mean that he or she is reluctant to discuss them with a third party, particularly in a work context.

The skilful counsellor will therefore explore all the issues as widely and discursively as possible, avoid drawing early conclusions, and listen carefully to what is said, to how it is expressed, and, in some cases, perhaps also to what is not being said. If the manager feels any doubts about the possible nature or causes of the absence, it may well at this stage also be appropriate to seek further expert or professional input before proceeding further. As a minimum, we would recommend that the manager should again review the case with relevant HR staff before taking any action. In many cases, though, there may be significant doubt about, for example, the precise mix of medical and non-medical causes, or about the genuineness of the stated causes. On such occasions it will generally be appropriate to seek the advice of professional occupational health advisers.

We would strongly recommend that any organisation trying seriously to address absence issues should obtain continuing access to skilled occupational health advice. Larger organisations may be in a position to employee an in-house physician, but there are a number of specialist operators in this field, as well as many GPs, who will provide this kind of service on a retained basis for employers. The role of the occupational health adviser is specifically to provide a source of independent, expert guidance in interpreting the available evidence. It is important to bear in mind that, in general, the occupational health adviser will not be in a position to come up with a definitive assessment or diagnosis in any specific case because he or she will not have access to the individual's medical history and records. However, a professional occupational health adviser will be able to help you assess, for example, whether a given pattern of absence is likely to be consistent with a particular medical condition, or whether the available evidence suggests some additional underlying factor that has not yet been identified. Above all, the occupational health adviser should be able to advise on whether additional information is required, and if so, on the most appropriate sources of advice.

Generally, if there are apparent medical causes for recurrent absence, it will be necessary to seek the individual's permission to approach his or her GP for a medical report. Indeed, as we noted in detail in Chapter 4, *it will ordinarily be appropriate to seek a report from the individual's GP before taking any significant action in respect of absence levels*, particularly if it may lead to formal disciplinary processes or even dismissal. This is partly a legal consideration, as set out in Chapter 4, but it is also simply a matter of good management practice. If you act on the basis of a full understanding of the circumstances, you are much more likely to take appropriate action to address the realities of the particular case. Having obtained the GP's report, therefore, it might also be appropriate to seek further expert input, particularly if the medical considerations are not clear-cut – for example, in cases that are stress-related or that appear to have some non-physical cause.

Nevertheless, no matter how much information and evidence is sought, experience indicates that decisions on handling absence are rarely straightforward and require a significant level of judgement. You may need to weigh up the evidence provided by the GP, by your own occupational health advisers and by other experts, alongside your own requirements as an employer. In many cases, the expert input, although valuable, may still be relatively non-committal – it may, for instance, be difficult for a GP, who may only see the patient occasionally, to provide a definitive judgement on his or her state of health. Even where there are clearly genuine health factors affecting attendance, you will still have to judge whether they appear to justify the levels of absence and whether any action might be taken to alleviate the problem.

Taking action

Having weighed up all the available evidence, therefore, the manager must gauge what action is appropriate as a response to the problem. The key objective here should simply be to address the absence issue, and you should consider any appropriate steps that may help to achieve this end. Formal action on the grounds of discipline or incapability must generally be a last resort, unless there are very strong reasons for taking immediate action. The starting-point will normally be a constructive discussion with the individual, building on the absence counselling process, which aims to identify practical steps that could be taken to improve attendance. The nature and mix of these steps will depend entirely on the apparent requirements of the specific case – but possible actions might include:

☐ the provision of medical or similar support which might help the employee to resolve an underlying or recurrent problem – To take a simple example, the recurrence of minor ailments might be indicative of generally poor health which could be addressed by changes in diet or lifestyle. In more extreme cases, it might be appropriate to provide support in dealing with some kind of addiction problem.

☐ discussing and agreeing specific changes in lifestyle, which might reduce recurrent problems (for example, the employee who regularly suffers minor injuries through sport) – In this kind of case, the employee should be advised that although the employer does not generally interfere with employees' activities outside the workplace, these may become a concern if they are repeatedly affecting the employee's ability to attend work. It is therefore reasonable to explore with the individual what steps might be taken to reduce the risk of non-attendance – for instance, by reducing the level or intensity of sporting activity or by adopting some alternative, less demanding pursuit.

☐ exploring sources of support and/or advice which might alleviate factors that may be affecting attendance – for example, if absence appears to be stress-related, it may be possible to identify support in areas such as financial or domestic responsibilities which would reduce the individual's stress levels outside work.

☐ considering logistical issues relating to the individual's working hours or location – If the individual is working very 'unsocial' hours or has a lengthy journey to work, for example, this might be affecting either his or her overall health or – from a slightly more sceptical perspective – his or her enthusiasm to attend work. It may or may not be possible to resolve these issues, but it is worth considering whether any options are available for transferring the individual to a different location or different working hours.

☐ reviewing the nature and level of the individual's role – If the individual has a particularly demanding role in the organisation, in terms of factors such as stress, concentration, unpredictability, physical demands, and so on, it may be that this is affecting his or her capability or motivation to attend work. Again, these issues may or may not be resolvable, but you should investigate any options for addressing such problems.

In exploring these and similar options, your aim should be to identify any reasonable steps that might be taken by the organisation to support the individual in improving his or her attendance. This does not mean that you are presenting the individual with a 'blank cheque' to make any desired changes – for instance, an employee cannot automatically expect to be able to change his or her working hours simply because this is more convenient domestically. But it should mean that you are providing any practical support that is consistent with the operational needs of the organisation.

Moreover, this is not a one-way contract. In parallel with exploring these constructive steps, you should be emphasising to the individual his or her own responsibilities for attending work. Depending on the circumstances of the case, it may also be appropriate to link any positive support with a tightening of the provisions surrounding absence. Examples might include:

☐ indicating to the individual that following the provision of additional support, the employer expects absence levels to improve across a defined time-scale. If this is not achieved, or if absence levels increase again in future, then the individual may expect to face more formal disciplinary action

☐ requiring the provision of a medical certificate for all absence

☐ requiring a periodic examination by the employer's

occupational health advisers to track progress in any health improvements.

This approach is likely to be particularly helpful in cases where there is some reasonable doubt about the legitimacy of the stated reasons for absence. It may be, for example, that the stated medical reasons for absence are genuine, but that their impact on attendance is being exaggerated.

Regardless of the mix of actions that are taken in a particular case, it is essential that monitoring continues over an extended period, and involves regular reviews of progress with the individual. The frequency of these reviews will depend on the nature of the problems and the actions being taken, but initially it is generally appropriate to meet with the individual on at least a monthly basis. The discussion should review actions being taken, and assess whether these appear to be having the desired effect on absence levels. If absence levels have not improved, it will be necessary to explore the reasons for that, and then to take any further action needed, including consideration of formal disciplinary action.

Organisation-wide initiatives and provisions

In the first part of this chapter we outlined the steps needed to implement effective absence management for individuals in the organisation. Our experience in practice is that the key to effective absence management generally lies in the interaction between managers and their teams. Absence managed effectively at this level, supported by a clear and appropriate framework of policies and procedures, will generally produce a significant improvement in attendance levels. Conversely, if absence is not being managed systematically and effectively at the individual level, there is likely to be no 'quick fix' available simply through the application of some organisation-wide policy or practice.

Nevertheless, as we have indicated in previous chapters, the application of organisation-wide principles or initiatives is likely to provide powerful reinforcement for managers' efforts in managing absence among their own staff. It is essential, therefore, that any comprehensive absence-management policy addresses both the skills and contribution of operational managers, and the broader HR initiatives or practices that might be needed both to support local activity and to address any endemic organisational issues.

Communication

First, once the overall absence management policy has been defined and agreed by the organisational steering group, it must be thoroughly and consistently communicated to the workforce as a whole. Commonly, absence management is seen as a stand-alone issue which is published in a discrete policy document but which is not reflected in broader HR materials or publications. In reality, attendance at work is a key issue which should lie at the heart of much HR and people management practice.

On this basis, therefore, the absence-management policies and procedures should be regularly publicised among the workforce, and reiterated in any relevant documentation. This might include terms and conditions, employee handbooks, induction materials, notice-boards, and so on. If the message is repeated clearly and simply, employers and managers will recognise that this is not simply a 'bolt-on', but a genuine priority to the organisation.

Alongside this, it may be helpful to produce regular organisational statistics of absence levels and targets across the organisation. An increasing number of organisations, recognising the real cost of absence, are beginning to see this as a key performance indicator, to be measured and publicised alongside more conventional measures of organisational performance. This includes the presentation of absence figures as part of the overall management data at senior management and board levels.

It may also be helpful to publish 'league tables' of absence levels across different areas of the business (or comparing absence levels with those in similar external organisations). As always, such 'league tables' must be treated with a degree of caution, because they can inspire unhealthy competitiveness that may lead to inappropriate action. Nevertheless, they can provide a powerful incentive to employees and management to improve performance and standards. It is often the case, for example, that employees simply do not recognise that their absence levels are significantly higher than those of their colleagues or of counterparts elsewhere. Highlighting these differences, therefore, can often be a valuable first step to breaking down entrenched cultures or practices.

Recruitment, selection and induction

As we noted in Chapter 3, effective procedures at the recruitment and induction stages can help to minimise the risk of importing individual absence problems into the organisation. Increasingly, organisations are introducing pre-employment health examinations for new recruits, although clearly there is an associated cost if examinations are provided for all prospective joiners. Also in Chapter 3 we mentioned that one option is to introduce a pre-employment questionnaire, perhaps supplemented by an interview with the organisation's occupational health adviser, which would identify the need for a more formal examination.

It is also important that questions of individual health and attendance are explored in job application forms, in interviews and in references, alongside issues such as travel to work requirements and any other factors likely to cause attendance problems. Nevertheless, it is important to recognise that these are sensitive issues which, if handled inappropriately, may potentially lead the employer into a risk of discrimination, particularly on the grounds of gender or disability. It is reasonable for the employer to state the standards of attendance that are expected in the organisation and to seek appropriate reassurance that these can be achieved. It is not reasonable for the employer to make any assumptions about, for example, potential attendance problems based on particular applicant characteristics or circumstances. Moreover, in exploring these areas, the employer should be prepared to take any reasonable steps that might facilitate attendance by an individual applicant, particularly with regard to applicants who have disabilities. Nevertheless, if these issues can be explored openly at this stage, it may be possible both to set clear standards and to offer any appropriate support before problems arise.

Performance management, reward and incentives

It is critical that absence-management policies are defined consistently throughout all aspects of HR practice in the organisation. It is perhaps surprising, for example, that relatively few organisations address absence levels explicitly in their performance management and appraisal systems, or incorporate consideration of absence into their performance-related pay structures. In practice, absence tends to be considered a performance issue only when it reaches a relatively extreme level.

However, in implementing an overall absence-management policy, it may be appropriate to include explicit consideration of absence records as part of the appraisal review. This would, as a minimum, provide a formal opportunity and requirement for managers to review the absence records of all their staff, allowing the issue to be discussed within the wider context of overall performance. This in turn would enable managers to discuss emerging absence issues (for example, instances where absence was increasing but not yet at problem levels) in a relatively non-threatening context. It would also provide an explicit demonstration to employees that the organisation was treating absence as a priority issue, alongside other aspects of performance.

In the same way, it may also be appropriate explicitly to consider, as part of the appraisal process, managers' handling of absence in their own area. Absence levels, for example, might be included as one of the basket of measures against which individual management performance is evaluated. A number of organisations have adopted variations on the 'balanced scorecard' approach, including consideration of 'people management' as well as more conventional measures of business performance. In this context, absence levels are likely to be a key consideration, alongside factors such as staff turnover and employee satisfaction. Again, it is important that these factors are not treated over-simplistically, and it may be necessary to review performance on both a quantitative and a qualitative basis. A manager may reduce absence levels in the short term by adopting a heavily punitive approach, but that is unlikely to produce lasting benefits for the organisation.

As we noted in Chapter 3, the linking of pay to attendance is a more controversial issue, and there is certainly a risk that the traditional 'attendance bonus' (in which some form of incentive is paid for achieving defined levels of attendance) is construed as, in effect, paying for attendance twice. Nevertheless, from a pragmatic perspective, there is no doubt that attendance bonuses can be effective, although the increasing trend is to link them to the achievement of team or organisational absence-improvement targets, rather than simply paying for individual attendance. More generally, where there is some existing link between pay and performance, it is entirely reasonable to encourage managers and staff to perceive attendance as one of the key contributors to individual and collective performance. After all, if an employee is not at work, for whatever reason, he or she is by definition not performing! It may therefore be appropriate to make any performance-related payment contingent on the achievement of acceptable attendance levels, as well as other performance measures. Similarly, it may be appropriate to include absence-management targets, alongside factors such as productivity or profitability, in any organisation-wide performance-improvement schemes.

It is also, of course, essential to consider the impact of any occupational sick-pay scheme on absence levels in the organisation. We discussed aspects of this in some detail in Chapter 3, notably those cases where occupational sick pay was seen as an entitlement that, in practice, actively encouraged higher levels of absence. We highlighted some cases where employers had tried to reduce provisions, both to cut costs and to encourage improved attendance. We also identified some instances where more generous provisions had been offered in exchange for achieving reduced absence levels.

In reality, this is always a difficult balance. Most good employers would want to offer reasonable provision to staff who are genuinely sick. At the same time, such provision clearly risks encouraging less scrupulous employees to take advantage of the organisation, and there appears to be no simple formula for reducing this risk. Experience indicates that, as so often, this is primarily an issue of effective management. It is important, therefore, that any scheme allows for payment to be withheld or reduced at management's discretion. On this basis the occupational sick scheme can be utilised as one of the tools available to managers in their handling of individual cases. In instances of recurrent short-term absence, for example, it may be possible for occupational sick pay to be withheld or made subject to the provision of medical certificates. It may also be possible for the provision of occupational sick pay to be made subject to the individual's undertaking some form of appropriate support, such as addiction counselling. It is notable that one of our case study organisations, James Cropper plc, established a rigorous absence-management procedure but then concluded that further improvements were likely to be dependent on changes to sick-pay arrangements and on some form of payment linked to attendance.

Work organisation and job design

As noted in Chapter 3, there is strong evidence that high absence levels are often linked to issues of employee commitment and motivation. This in turn may be linked to factors such as low levels of job satisfaction, lack of job variety, or absence of employee involvement or empowerment. If, therefore, there is an endemic absence problem in the organisation or part of the organisation which, on the basis of the available evidence, seems to be linked to these factors, we should consider issues of work design as part of the overall absence-management policy.

In practice, some care may be required in this area. Although there may be very good general reasons for restructuring roles or work activities, this may not necessarily be an initial priority in terms of absence management. If the key priority is to reduce absence levels, practical results are more likely to be achieved through investment in the quality of policies, procedures and individual management, as described in the first part of this chapter, rather than in large-scale re-engineering of activities. The potential benefits of such re-engineering may well be substantial, but are likely to be longer-term and wider-ranging, and may well require relatively high levels of investment.

Nevertheless, in the longer term, if problems of work design are not addressed, they are likely to prove a continuing barrier to achieving the highest levels of performance – in attendance as in other aspects of operational effectiveness. In parallel with more targeted investment for improving absence management, therefore, it is likely to be appropriate to consider factors such as:

- □ what might be done to reduce or eliminate our requirement for highly routine jobs, or to provide more variety through job rotation or broadening the range of tasks in a specific job
- □ what scope there is for enhancing employee involvement in job-related decision-making and providing more empowerment
- □ whether we could restructure or decentralise the organisation so as to create more employee identity with a sub-unit of activity
- □ what scope there is for introducing teamworking, allied to multiskilling and greater mutual interdependence of roles, enhancing attendance motivation through commitment to the team
- □ what scope there is for increasing commitment and motivation through training and development, providing more opportunities to learn new skills or offering career-development opportunities through internal promotion.

In short, it is likely that good HR and management practice will have a positive impact on attendance, just as they will on other aspects of employee performance. From a management perspective, therefore, it is critical that any focus on absence management does not become overly mechanical or one-dimensional. While there is no doubt that the immediate key to effective absence management lies primarily in the handling of individual and team issues, it is also true that longer-term benefits are likely to be achieved only within the context of positive overall employment and people management practices.

Flexible employment policies

There is no doubt that, in practice, a significant portion of absence in organisations results from personal or domestic issues rather than from genuine medical causes (although, as we indicated in the earlier part of this chapter, the distinction is not always clear-cut). In reality we all face tensions between our work and our domestic responsibilities, and for some employees this results in conflicts which can be resolved only through the use of supposed 'sickness absence'. Ironically, in many organisations, this is the only 'acceptable' way of taking time off work at short notice – the organisation may treat lateness as a disciplinary matter, and only grant annual leave on more extended notice. As a result, the employee who needs to take an hour off to deal with some domestic crisis has, in effect, no choice but to telephone in sick for the whole day!

Although of course it is ultimately the employee's responsibility to ensure that he or she is in a position to attend work as required, many employers now recognise that a greater degree of flexibility, supported by appropriate control mechanisms, is likely to produce benefits for all parties. Such provisions are also increasingly being considered within the context of helping employees to improve their work–life balance or promoting a more family-friendly approach to employment.

Again, the appropriate mix of provisions will depend both on the general needs and characteristics of the organisation, and the available evidence about the causes of absence. Potential options include:

☐ developing flexitime arrangements, particularly in areas where predictability of resourcing levels is not essential

☐ responding flexibly to requests for full-timers to transfer to part-time work or to job-share in order to accommodate other, non-work responsibilities

☐ allowing individual shifts or patterns of work which differ from standard hours, or indeed constructing general working patterns which might fit within non-work responsibilities (such as shifts which operate within school hours)

- developing formal homeworking or teleworking initiatives, or simply providing more flexibility to allow employees to work from home occasionally.

In addition, the organisation might take steps to 'legitimise' absence for domestic or personal reasons. This might include (as in the Scottish Prison Service case study, for example) broadening the categories of 'special leave' which can be taken at management's discretion. One organisation, for example, introduced improved provisions for 'carer' leave, which allowed staff to take a defined amount of time off, at management discretion, to deal with such responsibilities. Another introduced 'emergency leave' provisions, which allowed employees to take a defined number of hours off without notice (for example, to allow a late start for domestic reasons), so long as a portion of the time was made up at a later date.

Occupational health initiatives

Alongside the various management initiatives described above, it may also be appropriate to take more general steps to help improve general employee health, or to provide health screening or preventative services. Again, the value and relevance of such initiatives will largely depend on the identified causes of absence in the organisation. Possible options here include:

- the development of stress-management policies and practices – These might include introducing stress audits to help measure the levels and causes of stress in the organisation, as well as potential initiatives designed to address any problems.

- improvements to working conditions and environment, particularly if employees are expected to work in physically demanding situations – Moreover, although we have not specifically considered health and safety issues in this book, clearly improvements in such standards and practices are also likely to have a positive impact on absence levels.

- the introduction of employee assistance and counselling

programmes – The availability of employee assistance schemes, through anonymous telephone helplines, may be a valuable means of encouraging employees to raise potential problems – particularly external or domestic factors, which may be difficult to raise within the organisation – before they begin to affect their attendance.

☐ implementation and support of policies in areas such as smoking and substance abuse

☐ health-screening programmes or services, such as 'well women' or 'well men' clinics

☐ provision of or support for gym, work-out or sports facilities.

Clearly, all of these provisions have associated costs, and the organisation will have to consider carefully the potential benefits. In all these cases, of course, the resulting benefits may be wider than simply a reduction in absence levels, in terms of employee commitment, motivation and overall productivity. More specifically, if these initiatives are introduced as part of a comprehensive absence-management programme which also includes the development and implementation of more rigorous absence procedures, they give a very visible demonstration of the organisation's willingness to tackle the issue from all perspectives. Both of our case study organisations, the Scottish Prison Service and James Cropper plc, introduced positive occupational health initiatives which provide a useful illustration of the range of approaches that can be adopted.

Conclusion

In the course of this book we have considered absence from a variety of perspectives, in particular its measurement and costing, its causes, methods of control, the legal perspective, and the implementation of policy initiatives.

Against this background, the current level of absence need not be accepted as an inevitable fact of organisational life. Of course people become ill, but the wide variations in absence levels experienced by different organisations, even within the same industry, cannot be explained simply by illness. Except in certain exceptional industries, good or bad employee health must be assumed to be normally distributed amongst different employee populations. As we stated in our Introduction, therefore, variations in absence levels must in large part result from differences in the actions taken by the organisational management. In the field of absence management, as in many others, the HR practitioner has a major contribution to make.

The key to a professional approach involves:

☐ benchmarking best practice
☐ aiming to match performance with the best rather than with just the average
☐ setting targets for achievement and monitoring to check that they are being met
☐ taking on board the idea of continuous improvement by setting progressively higher targets.

Above all, though, effective absence management requires a comprehensive and balanced approach, tailored to the needs and characteristics of the organisation. It must ensure the rigorous and systematic management of individual cases, supported by constructive initiatives and incentives that actively support improved attendance.

APPENDIX 1: CASE STUDIES

James Cropper plc

James Cropper plc is a major manufacturer of coloured and specialist papers and related products, based in Burneside near Kendal, Cumbria. The company has operated from this site since 1845 and remains very much a dominant presence in the local community as the major employer in the area. It has a strong reputation for product quality, operating at the high-quality end of the paper manufacturing market. In recent years it has continued to develop and innovate to meet the needs of this highly demanding and competitive marketplace. Developments included a substantial programme of re-equipment in the 1980s and 1990s, alongside a continuing drive to improve production efficiency and quality, and to enhance the motivation, commitment and productivity of the workforce.

At the same time, the company has also retained a strong sense of its own history, traditions and values, as well as continuing links with the founding Cropper family. The current chairman, also called James Cropper, is a great-grandson of the company's founder. The company has always been aware of its responsibilities as a local employer, and of the need to develop and sustain working practices to enable it to remain competitive in a volatile industry. It also recognises the benefits of maintaining a strong company culture, with a focus on teamworking and commitment to the company's success. Continuing efforts have been made over the last decade to create a more proactive and empowered workforce, the employees being encouraged and supported to take increasing responsibility for driving company performance.

Against this background, James Cropper plc has in recent years been devoting increasing attention to the management of absence within the business. The company has applied the key principles of absence management, as examined in preceding chapters, in order to establish a rigorous foundation for reducing absence across the organisation. At the same time it has recognised that these may have to be reinforced by the introduction of some more radical changes in order to address long-established attitudes to absence.

Prior to the introduction of the new arrangements, the company recognised that absence levels had traditionally been relatively high, and that this was adding a substantial bottom-line cost to the business. The chief executive, Alun Lewis, points out that in an industry where margins are customarily extremely tight, factors such as absence have a substantial impact on productivity and therefore profitability. The company has estimated that on an annual basis, each 1 per cent of absence costs the company in the region of £100,000 on the bottom line. With absence in the year 2000 running at around 6.4 per cent, therefore, he identified an opportunity to produce substantial improvements in overall business performance.

In line with the principles set out in Chapter 5, the first stage was to understand the nature of the issues facing the company in respect of absence. In fact, the company had for some years operated a formal absence policy which, at least in theory, reflected much of the best practice described in the earlier chapters of this book. It included, for example, a clear statement of the company's policy and principles in respect of absence, definitions of the respective roles of the line manager and HR, systematic procedures for dealing with persistent short-term absence, a framework for conducting return-to-work interviews, and so on. However, despite the quality of this underpinning material, its practical application by managers was extremely variable. There was, for example, evidence that managers were in some cases failing to confront problems of short-term persistent sickness, and there were also some instances where longer-term sickness absence had caused operational difficulties that had not been effectively resolved. These weaknesses in the management of absence were also linked to some more positive aspects of the company's traditional culture and values. The company had tended to operate a very supportive approach to dealing with employees who were absent through sickness, and (for example) had in place some very generous provisions for sick pay. It was recognised, therefore, that there was a need to retain many of the positive values that had characterised the company's previous practices, but to establish a much more rigorous approach to managing absence.

With this in mind, the company reviewed the scale of its absence problem against industry averages, in order to reinforce its messages to the workforce and the trade unions about the opportunity to reduce absence levels. Initially, the company drew on the 2000 CBI Absence Survey, which reported an average absence level of 4.0 per cent among manual employees and 2.8 per cent among non-manual employees. By comparison, James Cropper plc's 2000 absence levels stood at 6.4 per cent among process employees and, more encouragingly, 2.1 per cent among non-process staff. This confirmed that, as expected, there was a significant opportunity to reduce absence levels among the process group.

So at the start of 2001 the company introduced a much more rigorous approach to the management of absence. The first step was a revision and 'relaunch', through discussion with the trade unions and with support from ACAS, of the company's absence policy. This defined, in clear and simple terms, the company's attitudes to absence:

> Absenteeism can seriously affect Company profitability and productivity. Although some absence is inevitable, levels can be reduced by the implementation of positive and consistent policies. An overall Company approach to absence will minimise disruption caused by absenteeism, and ensure that employees are treated fairly.

This policy was then underpinned by a set of clearly defined principles, including:

- [ ] clear communication of rules and procedures concerning absence to all staff
- [ ] the need for consistency and uniformity in the application of these rules and procedures
- [ ] the requirement for return-to-work interviews following all absences
- [ ] the role of the HR function in ensuring consistency and providing support for managers as required.

In parallel with introducing these revised absence procedures, the company provided training for managers and supervisors in the management of absence and the conducting of return-to-work interviews. The company also used its HR Information System to support more rigorous management and monitoring of absence, to identify those instances where persistent absence appeared to be a problem. This also enabled the HR function to review the application of the absence-management policies to ensure that they were being applied systematically and consistently across the organisation.

As a result of these new procedures, return-to-work interviews were conducted consistently following all absences, regardless of the causes or duration. This in turn enabled each absence to be effectively categorised, enabling individual cases to be handled appropriately. This meant, for example, that cases could be referred to the company's occupational health advisers where appropriate, and that cases of persistent absenteeism could be rapidly identified and dealt with. Where there was evidence of recurrent absence, the case was escalated into a formal procedure, with a range of staged interventions. These might include, at appropriate stages, formal warnings, the involvement of HR, loss of entitlement to company sick pay, and, in extreme cases, dismissal on the grounds of insufficient capability.

In parallel with this more rigorous management of individual absence, the company also took steps to deal with several outstanding instances of long-term or recurrent absence. In a small number of cases, this resulted in termination of employment on the grounds of insufficient capability or in voluntary early retirement, each case being handled sensitively in line with the company's overall values and standards. In addition, the company took the opportunity at this stage to reduce the level of sick pay provision for new joiners to the company. Previously, the level of provision had been considerably higher than the industry norms. Although the new provisions were still in line with industry best practice, they were set at a level more appropriate to the company's competitive position in the marketplace.

The company also took a number of steps to provide positive support in healthcare matters. These have included, in recent years, campaigns to reduce smoking and promote healthier lifestyles, support in physiotherapy for back-related or similar problems, and efforts to encourage healthier diets.

However, despite these various initiatives during 2001, the overall impact on absence levels has so far been relatively limited. The absence levels for process staff fell slightly from 6.4 per cent in 2000 to 6.2 per cent in 2001 (whereas, according to the CBI survey, overall absence levels among manual employees rose slightly over that period), and absence levels for non-process staff stayed static. This was a disappointment to the business, but there was a recognition that the impact of more rigorous approaches might take longer to become fully evident. There is confidence now that the foundations have been established, with consistent and systematic management in place, for absence levels to continue to be reduced.

Nevertheless, in the light of the absence statistics for 2001, the company has decided that further and more radical action will be needed over the coming year and beyond, in order to reinforce the absence management procedures. As we recommended in Chapter 5, the company has now set very clear targets for the absence management processes – namely, the reduction of absence levels by at least 2 per cent. More generally, the company's aim is to reduce the costs incurred through absenteeism, while continuing to manage the business in line with its traditional values of fairness and consistency.

The company is currently in the process of finalising and negotiating new grading and pay arrangements, with the aim of achieving single-status conditions across the business as a whole. As part of these negotiations, James Cropper plc is also looking to revise its overall sick-pay procedures to establish terms more appropriate to the company's current business needs.

Although the precise impact of this has not yet been finalised, Alun Lewis's overall objective is that 'the blank cheque approach should end'. In other words, the company wishes to establish terms which are fair to employees but which do not provide excessively generous or open-ended support for employees who are not attending work. To this end, the company wishes to bring sick pay provision for all employees into line with the terms that have now been agreed for new starters. Currently, employees can receive up to 12 months' sick leave at 100 per cent of their normal pay, plus a further six months' at 50 per cent. The arrangements for new starters, by contrast, link entitlement to length of service, but with an upper limit of only 26 weeks.

Perhaps more radically, the company is also seeking to introduce a scheme whereby only the first five days' absence in any given calendar year would attract 100 per cent of contractual pay. Any subsequent absence would attract only 75 per cent of contractual pay. However, it would be possible for staff to accumulate 'unused' sickness absence to improve their entitlement to sick pay in subsequent years. For example, an employee who had had no sickness absence for five years would then be entitled to up to 25 days at full pay. Alun Lewis comments:

> The aim is to be fair to both the employee and to the business. I think it's entirely reasonable that an employee who has a good track record of attendance over a long period should receive more generous provision if they are then forced to be absent for genuine reasons.

Conversely, if an employee has had a track record of recurrent medium- or long-term absence, this might result in a loss of overall sick-pay entitlement. For example, the company is considering whether sick-pay entitlement should be constrained within a rolling three-year timescale – so, for example, entitlement could be withdrawn from an employee who had taken more than 26 weeks in any three-year period.

More positively, the company is also considering options for introducing some form of attendance-linked bonus. This might be a straightforward payment linked to attendance, or might comprise an element of the performance-related bonus scheme being proposed as part of the new grading and pay arrangements. The company is keen to emphasise that in practice, attendance is an aspect of performance – after all, if an employee is not at work, he or she is not performing.

The nature and detail of these provisions is still to be finalised, and will be subject to negotiation with the company's trade unions. The unions are of course concerned about the content and application of these provisions, although there is a general recognition of the need to manage absence effectively in order both to reduce costs and to ensure that employees are all being treated fairly. Most importantly, in line with the principles set out in Chapter 7, the company is continuing to adopt a comprehensive and dynamic approach to the management of absence. Having built a foundation of rigorous procedures, James Cropper plc is now aiming to develop this further by addressing the pay and other structural factors perceived to be affecting attendance levels adversely. This is seen as the start of a continuing process that will be reviewed on an annual basis in order to ensure that the procedures remain appropriate and are being consistently and effectively applied.

The Scottish Prison Service

The Scottish Prison Service (SPS) employs over 4,500 staff currently based across 15 establishments ranging in size from Barlinnie in Glasgow, which houses around 1,000 prisoners, to Porterfield in Inverness, which accommodates just over 100. In addition, the Service has its Headquarters at Calton House in Edinburgh, and operates the Scottish Prison Service College in Polmont. Around three quarters of the staff are Prison Officers across various categories.

The Service has traditionally suffered from relatively high absence levels, which at one stage in the late 1980s ran at nearly 30 days per employee. In part this reflected the stresses and pressures associated with the nature of the environment and work. In addition, absence levels in the past reflected a history of generally poor industrial relations and low staff morale. Over a number of years a culture had been established within which a level of sickness absence was seen as 'acceptable'.

During the early 1990s, in the face of increasingly demanding operational and performance requirements, the SPS began to embark on a programme of organisational and culture change, with the aim of supporting the Service's ambitious mission and vision statements. The Service's key aims are defined as:

☐ custody

☐ order

☐ care

☐ opportunity.

These aims are in turn underpinned by five main themes:

☐ leadership in correctional service

☐ a prison estate that is fit for the purpose

☐ highest standards of service

☐ respect for staff

☐ value for money for the taxpayer.

From a human resources perspective, one of the first steps towards these objectives was the establishment of a more professional and focused HR service, capable of providing effective support for operational and line managers within local establishments. This involved the decentralisation of the HR function, which had previously focused on providing a largely administrative service from Headquarters, with the appointment of CIPD-qualified HR managers and staff within each establishment. It was part of a wider objective of increasing local empowerment and accountability for performance.

Against this background the management of absence was seen as a major priority, the SPS recognising its significant impact on establishment costs and productivity. In 1994 the Service introduced a new national set of guidelines for the management of absence, which were agreed with the trade unions as the basis for local implementation. The intention was to ensure a much more systematic approach to the handling of individual absence. This included the use of return-to-work interviews and increasing use of formal absence counselling when absence levels reached defined trigger-points.

These local interventions initially produced significant improvements in absence levels, enabling the Service to reduce them from an average of around 18.6 shifts lost per employee per year to around 14. However, further improvements proved difficult, and the local implementation of absence policies and practices was very variable. In particular, there was a lack of good information on absence levels and patterns to inform both local interventions and national monitoring. It was therefore decided that the SPS had to build on these foundations by developing a more systematic, nationally-supported framework for managing absence.

The first step was to establish a foundation of reliable management information to enable the Service to identify and respond appropriately to absence issues and trends. This involved distilling the existing categories for recording absence causes, which had been over-complex and uninformative, into simpler and more meaningful groupings. Using the resulting management information, the SPS then worked in consultation with the trade unions to develop a new national framework for managing sickness absence across the Service.

From this point the aim was to establish new attitudes to absence, challenging the culture that perceived sickness absence as an 'entitlement'. Secondly, there was standardisation of the trigger-points for a warning across all SPS locations (the triggers being three periods of absence, nine days of sick absence in any rolling period of 12 months, or any discernible pattern of absence that gave cause for concern). This in turn required more systematic analysis and management of absence levels – including the application of the 'Bradford factor' formula (see Chapter 1, page 7) – to define parameters for management discretion, with a particular focus on dealing with short-term and persistent absence. The intention was to ensure consistency of approach across all the establishments while still supporting local flexibility in addressing specific issues or requirements. To this end local managers were given discretion in the handling of individual absence until a defined 'Bradford factor' formula score was reached. Beyond this point a formal warning would automatically be initiated, and the case would be handled through a series of defined procedures.

The trigger-points and 'Bradford factor' scores are monitored by local HR managers within each establishment, who then initiate the required action with local operational managers. The scores are currently calculated and triggered manually, although the SPS is about to introduce a new HR Information System which will trigger the process automatically. It is also hoped that the new system will improve central monitoring of absence trends across the Service as a whole.

Except in cases where there has been a transparent breach of discipline (eg where an employee has not followed the internal procedures), no judgement is made about the legitimacy of the incidents of absence. However, the procedure stresses that any avoidable absence is unacceptable to the organisation, and that every reasonable step should be taken to ensure attendance. This is underpinned both by rigorous management of individual cases and by the provision of positive support where appropriate. At the launch of the programme, operational and HR managers were taken through an extensive programme of training in absence counselling and management to ensure that they had the skills to support delivery of the new procedures.

Return-to-work meetings are held as a matter of course following any incidence of absence. The purpose of the interview is to ensure full understanding of the reasons for the individual's absence, to facilitate the individual's return to work, and to minimise the likelihood of any future associated absence. Once a trigger-point has been breached (subject to any discretion exercised within the 'Bradford factor' score limits), the individual is automatically called to an absence interview and a formal absence warning is issued. From this point, if the absence problem persists, the individual is taken through a formal procedure with staged warnings and the possibility – if the problem cannot be resolved – of dismissal on the grounds of insufficient capability. Formal appeals are allowed at every stage in this process, and if dismissal is required, compensation under Civil Service Pension Rules may be paid to the individual concerned.

While this procedure is rigorously managed, the SPS does of course provide positive support in resolving the causes of the absence problem. This is likely to include referral to the SPS's occupational health advisers in order that they may identify any practical steps that can be taken to help improve the individual's attendance.

Alongside this rigorous management of individual cases, the SPS has also taken a number of broader positive steps to improve the overall health and fitness of its workforce. These have included:

☐ improvements in pre-employment medical checks to ensure that any issues are identified and addressed at the earliest opportunity – the SPS works within the provisions of the Disability Discrimination Act in handling individual recruitment or employment issues, although at present prison officers are formally exempt from the Act's requirements

□ the introduction of formal annual fitness testing for those recruited into operational roles, as well as improved provision of medical examinations

□ the outsourcing of occupational health provision for the SPS – since 1999 this has ensured a consistency of service and quality with regard to occupational health provision for all employees in the organisation

□ a computerised health and welfare software package – this has been provided in all establishments, and allows staff access to health and fitness assessments on site

□ pilot schemes for providing physiotherapy support for establishments – the SPS is currently assessing the provision of on-site and local community clinics and the effects of this on the management of musculoskeletal disorders

□ the development of a stress management policy, underpinned by risk assessment guidelines to help identify causes of individual and organisational stress

□ the provision of well person clinics at individual locations

□ the development of proactive immunisation policies – eg immunisation against influenza available to all staff; immunisation against hepatitis B is being piloted on selected SPS sites

□ the introduction of an Employee Assistance Programme – this has been ongoing since 1998 and provides free, direct, confidential and unlimited access to a 24-hour helpline 365 days a year: employees can also access one-to-one counselling sessions

□ the development of policies which address substance and alcohol misuse and smoking – the organisation offers proactive assistance to staff who experience addiction issues.

Overall, the systematic management of absence in this way has produced substantial reductions in absence levels. The average number of shifts lost per employee per year has gone down from 18.6 to 10.2, and the Service now compares relatively well with appropriate external comparators. Above all, the SPS has established a culture in which absence is not seen as 'acceptable' or the norm. At the same time, although the process is undoubtedly highly rigorous, it is generally perceived as supportive rather than merely punitive.

Simultaneously, the SPS is not complacent and is working towards even more demanding targets for absence levels. The system continues to be improved. In particular, the SPS recognises that it needs more detailed and reliable data than is currently available, and it is expected that the new Information System will enable this. Efforts are also being made to improve consistency of practice and application. For example, the 'Bradford factor' score triggers can be suspended if the absence has occurred as a result of an injury at work or if it is stress-related (in these cases different procedures are applied). At present there appears to be some inconsistency in the application of these exemptions, so the SPS is reviewing the available data and practices to support a more consistent approach. The organisation is also aiming to improve its accident-reporting procedures to provide more comprehensive data to support both health and safety and absence management.

APPENDIX 2:
SOURCES OF TRAINING SUPPORT MATERIALS

Training support materials are available in the form of paper-based training exercises and videos. Products on the market include the following.

Paper-based training exercises

Daedal Training offer a package entitled *No Work Today – A Maze Exercise on Absenteeism*. This exercise comes in an A4 ring-binder and may be used either by individuals as a workbook or for group training purposes. The exercise opens with a brief scenario in which a supervisor is faced with a problem of repeated short-term absences on the part of an employee. Trainees are asked to select one from a range of options for action, and having made their selection, they are guided to another page of the binder where a further decision must be made from the options available. The decision-making exercise continues until the trainees have reached one of three outcomes: the resignation of the absent employee, the dismissal of the employee, or a resolution of the underlying cause of absence. It is designed as a 'maze' through which trainees travel according to their decisions. The trainer is provided with a map of the maze, which contains 'blind alleys' if certain routes are pursued and features a shortest route for those who make the appropriate decisions at each stage. It costs £145 and is available from Daedal Training Limited, Yateley Lodge, Reading Road, Yateley, Hampshire, GU46 7AA, (tel: 01252 862416; website: www.daedal-training.com).

Flex Learning Media offer a self-study workbook entitled *Attacking Absenteeism*, originally published in the United States. The workbook opens with some background information about the nature of absenteeism and then takes readers through a series of questionnaires to help assess how they currently deal with the problem at their workplace and determine what should be done in the future. It concludes with a number of case examples of successful absence-control programmes implemented in named American companies. The retail price is £9.95, with discounts for large quantities, and it can be obtained from Flex Learning Media, 9–15 Hitchen Street, Baldock SG7 6AL (tel: 01462 895544/896000; fax: 01462 892417; website: www.btinternet.com/-flex-learningmedia). The Company also provides a range of other materials of potential relevance to training in absence management, including 'Trainer Resource Packs', a video and a computer-based training programme in counselling skills. It is also planning to release a 'Trainer Resource Pack' on absenteeism.

Fenman Ltd have published an 'activity pack' containing 18 activities for inclusion in training programmes in attendance management for HR professionals and line managers. Written by Mark Briegel and entitled *Managing for Better Attendance*, the activity pack is available at £195 from Fenman Ltd, Clive House, The Business Park, Ely, Cambridgeshire CB7 4EH (tel: 01353 665533; fax: 01353 663644; e-mail: service@fenman.co.uk; website: www.fenman.co.uk).

Northgate Training provides a pack of trainer's notes, OHP slides, case-based materials and task sheets for participants entitled *Harry and Absenteeism*, one of a series of eight training packs based around various problems faced by a typical manager. The materials consist of background facts about absence in a section and require participants to use the task sheets provided to analyse and present their findings on the nature of these problems and how they might be tackled. The pack costs £95 and is available from Northgate Training, 29 James Street West, Bath BA1 2BT (tel: 01225 339733; fax: 01225 429151; e-mail: ngate@dial.pipex.com).

Videos

Connaught Training offer *Gone Today, Here Tomorrow*, a 20-minute video, and a 20-page trainer's guide highlighting the main learning-points in the film. The video contains two scenarios of roughly equal length, one set in a factory and the other in a shop. Both illustrate the importance of gathering the facts about employees' absences and give two examples of conducting absence-review discussions between managers and staff designed to agree action plans for improvement. The cost of purchase is £825 (five-day rental: £210; three-day rental: £160) from Connaught Training Limited,

Unit 2 (off Blackwater Way), Lower Farnham Road, Aldershot GU12 4DY (tel: 01235 331551 for hire, and 01235 827730 for purchase).

Merlin Communications offer a video training product entitled *Absence Management*. Just under 35 minutes in length, it contains four short scenarios on: proactive intervention designed to avoid absence, managing longer spells of sickness, conducting return-to-work interviews, and rehabilitating and helping the longer-term sick to return to work. Merlin Communications also specialise in providing videos and associated training handbooks for local government and the Health Service entitled *Managing Sickness Absence*. The videos and associated materials may be used both to support group training events and as open learning resource packs for line managers to take away and refer to when planning absence-review meetings. The company also offers a bespoke service for larger clients in which employees of the organisations can feature in the videos. The pack of two videos contains case examples of absence problems and looks in some depth at the role of absence policies and procedures and at the techniques of conducting return-to-work and absence-review interviews. The price per pack of two videos and support materials is £599.95 for 1–9 packs, £299.95 for 10–49 packs and £99.95 for 50 or more packs; licences are also available for customising the video. Merlin Communications (UK) Limited can be contacted at Dyer House, 3 Dyer Street, Cirencester GL7 2PP (tel: 01285 641851; fax: 01285 643164).

Fenman Training have produced a video and DVD entitled *Improving Attendance: What Managers Can Do*. Lasting around 20 minutes, it focuses on the conducting of return-to-work interviews and shows a range of different scenarios and absence problems being handled. The video/DVD also comes with a Trainer's Guide, which sets out the suggested content of one-hour and full-day sessions and includes pre-course worksheets, role play materials and visual aids. Fenman Training are located at Clive House, The Business Park, Ely, Cambridgeshire CB7 4EH (tel: 01353 665533; fax: 01353 663644; e-mail: service@fenman.co.uk; website: www.fenman.co.uk).

Training courses in absence management are offered by The Civil Service College (tel: 01344 634000), the Engineering Employers' Federation (tel: 01256 763969) and the Industrial Society (tel: 020 7839 4300); the latter has also produced a video.

BIBLIOGRAPHY

Advisory, Conciliation, and Arbitration Service (ACAS) (1999) *Absence and Labour Turnover*. London, ACAS.

Advisory, Conciliation, and Arbitration Service (ACAS) (2000a) *Code of Practice on Disciplinary Practice and Procedures in Employment*. London, HMSO.

Advisory, Conciliation, and Arbitration Service (ACAS) (2000b) *Discipline at Work*. London, ACAS.

Aiken O. (1996a) 'Ill-health dismissals'. *People Management*, 7 November. p.47.

Aiken O. (1996b) 'Who pays what when your employee falls ill?' *People Management*, 21 November. pp.46–47.

Aiken A. (1992) 'Conspicuous by their absence'. *PM Plus*, 3, 7, July. pp.20–21.

Arkin A. (1993) 'The workforce who got sick of absenteeism'. *PM Plus*, 4, 11, November. pp.18–19.

Arkin A. (1997) 'Behind the screens'. *People Management*, 7 November. pp.39–40.

Baltes B. B., Briggs T. E., Huff J. W., Wright J. A. *and* Newman G. A. (1999) 'Flexible and compressed workweek schedules: a meta analysis of their effect on work-related criteria', *Journal of Applied Psychology*, 84, 4, August. pp.496–513.

Barmby T., Ercolani M. *and* Treble J. (1999) 'Sickness absence in Great Britain: new quarterly and annual series from GHS and LFS, 1971–1997', *Labour Market Trends*, August. pp.405–415.

Beckard R. (1992) 'A model for the executive management of transformational change', in G. Salaman (ed.), *Human Resource Strategies*. London, Sage.

Bevan S. (2001) 'Counting the cost of absence', *IRS Employment Review*, No 739, 1 November. pp.46–47.

Bevan S. *and* Hayday S. (1998) *Absence Management: A review of good practice.* Report 353. Brighton, Institute of Employment Studies.

BEVAN S. *and* HAYDAY S. (2001) *Costing Sickness Absence in the UK.* Report 382. Brighton, Institute of Employment Studies.

BRAVERMAN H. (1974) *Labour and Monopoly Capital.* New York, Monthly Review Press.

BUCHANAN D. (1989) 'Job enrichment is dead: long live high performance work design', *Personnel Management*, May. pp.40–43.

BUCHANAN D. (1992) 'High performance: new boundaries of acceptability in worker control', in G. Salaman (ed.), *Human Resource Strategies.* London, Sage.

BUCHANAN D. (1994) 'Principles and practice in work design', in K. Sisson (ed.), *Personnel Management: A comprehensive guide to theory and practice in Britain.* Oxford, Blackwell.

CONFEDERATION OF BRITISH INDUSTRY (CBI) (1989) *Managing Absence.* London, CBI.

CBI (1993) *Too Much Time Out? CBI/Percom Survey on Absence from Work.* London, CBI.

CBI/Hay (1994) *People, Paybill and the Public Sector.* London CBI.

CBI/CENTREFILE (1995) *Managing Absence: 1995 CBI/Centrefile survey results.* London, CBI.

CBI/BUPA/MCG (1997) *Managing Absence: In sickness and in health.* London, CBI.

CBI/BUPA (1998) *Missing Out: 1998 Absence and labour turnover survey.* London, CBI.

CBI/BUPA (1999) *Focus on Absence: 1999 Absence and labour turnover survey.* London, CBI.

CBI/PPP (2000) *Focus on Absence: Absence and labour turnover survey 2000.* London, CBI.

CBI/PPP (2001) *Pulling Together: 2001 Absence and labour turnover survey.* London, CBI.

CCH (2000) 'Measuring absence', in *CCH Absence Manual.* Bicester, CCH Editions Ltd.

CCH (2001) 'Disability discrimination', in *British Personnel Management.* Bicester, CCH Editions Limited.

CIPD (2000) *Employee Absence: A survey of management policy and practice.* London, CIPD.

CIPD (2001) *Employee Absence: A survey of management policy and practice.* London, CIPD.

CRONER/CCH (2000) 'Absenteeism management and the DDA', *Employment Briefing*, Issue no 198, 11 Sept. pp.6–7.

COX S. (1999) 'Managing sickness absence within the law: part 1', *Occupational Health Review*, January/February. pp.33–35.

DALTON D. R. *and* MESCH D. J. (1990) 'The impact of flexible scheduling on employee attendance and turnover', *Administrative Science Quarterly*, 35. pp.370–387.

DONKIN R. (1998) 'How give and take yields results', *Financial Times*, 17 December. p.19.

DRAGO R. *and* WOODEN M. (1992) 'The determinants of labour absence: economic factors and workgroup norms across countries', *Industrial and Labor Relations Review*, 45, 4, July. pp.764–778.

DUNLEAVY R. (1999) 'Train firm offers cash for drivers not to be ill', *Daily Telegraph*, 16 February. p.9.

EDWARDS P. K. *and* WHISTON C. (1989) 'Industrial discipline, the control of attendance and the subordination of labour: towards an integrated analysis', *Work, Employment and Society*, Vol.3, No.1, March. pp.1–28.

EMPLOYERS' FORUM ON DISABILITY (2000) *A Practical Guide to Managing Sickness Absence*. London, Employers' Forum on Disability.

EVANS A. (1991) *Computers and Personnel Systems*. London, IPM.

EVANS A. (1998) *Family-Friendly Policies, Special Leave and the Parental Leave Directive*. Bicester, CCH.

EVANS A. (1999a) 'Managing absence in the public sector', *CCH Absence Newsletter*, Issue 14, April. pp.2–4.

EVANS A. (1999b) 'The role of computerised HR systems in absence management', *CCH Absence Newsletter*, Issue 16, June. pp 2–4.

EVANS A. (1999c) 'Training managers in absence: a review of employer's practices and training support materials on the market', *CCH Absence Newsletter*, Issue 18, September. pp.2–3.

EVANS A. (2000a) 'Rehabilitating the long-term sick at Marks & Spencer', *CCH Personnel Management Newsletter*, Issue 50, 24 March. pp.6–7.

EVANS A. (2000b) 'Absence management programme at Nottinghamshire County Council Social Services', *CCH Personnel Management Newsletter*, Issue 65, 27 November. pp.5–8.

EVANS A. (2001) *Staff Recruitment and Retention*. Oxford, Chandos.

EVANS A. *and* ATTEW T. (1986) 'Alternatives to full-time permanent staff', in C. Curson (ed.), *Flexible Patterns of Work*. London, IPM.

FAIR H. (1992) *Personnel and Profit*. London, IPM.

FOWLER A. (1993) *Discipline*. London, IPM.

FOWLER A. (1997) 'Benchmarking', *People Management*, 12 June. pp.39–40.

GEE (1999) *Absence: An audit of cost reduction procedures*. London, Gee Publishing.

GOLDMAN L. *and* LEWIS J. (1999) 'The problem of sickness absence', *Occupational Health*, April. pp.12–13.

GREATER LONDON EMPLOYERS' ASSOCIATION (1999) *Sickness Absence in the London Boroughs*. Benchmarking Report No 4, November. London, GLEA.

GRUNDEMANN R. W. M. *and* VAN VUUREN C. V. (1997) *Preventing Absenteeism at the Workplace*. Dublin, European Foundation for the Improvement of Living and Working Conditions.

HACKMAN J. R. *and* OLDHAM G. R. *et al* (1975) 'A new strategy for job enrichment', *California Management Review*, 17, 4. pp.57–71.

HALL H. (1998a) 'How disability discrimination law is affecting absence management', *CCH Absence Newsletter*, Issue 1, January. pp.2–4.

HALL H. (1998b) 'Handling absent employees at the end of maternity leave', *CCH Absence Newsletter*, Issue 3, March. pp.2–4.

HALL H. (1999) 'Absence and leave management: case law developments'. *CCH Absence Newsletter*, Issue 15, May. pp.2–4.

HALL H. (2000) 'Sick pay and long-term disability benefits – benefit or burden?', *CCH Absence Newsletter*, Issue 21, January. pp.1–4.

HARGREAVES S., MORTON G. *and* TAYLOR G. (1998) *Managing Absence: A handbook for managers in public and voluntary organisations*. Lyme Regis, Russell House.

HARVEY J. *and* NICHOLSON N. (1993) 'Incentives and penalties as a means of influencing attendance: a study in the UK public sector', *International Journal of Human Resource Management*, 4, 4, December.

HERZBERG F. (1966) *Work and the Nature of Man*. London, Staples Press.

HILL J. M. M. *and* TRIST E. L. (1953) 'A consideration of industrial accidents as a means of withdrawal from the work situation', *Human Relations*, 6. pp.357–380.

HILL J. M. M. *and* TRIST E. L. (1955) 'Changes in accidents and other absences with length of service', *Human Relations*, 8. pp.121–152.

HUCZYNSKI A. A. *and* FITZPATRICK M. J. (1989) *Managing Employee Absence for a Competitive Edge*. London, Pitman.

INCOMES DATA SERVICES (IDS) (1991) *Sick Pay Schemes*. Study 475, February.

INCOMES DATA SERVICES (IDS) (1992) *Controlling Absence*. Study No.498, January.

INCOMES DATA SERVICES (IDS) (1994a) 'Persistent absenteeism'. *IDS Brief*, No.516, May. pp.7–10.

INCOMES DATA SERVICES (IDS) (1994b) *Absence and Sick Pay Policies*. Study No.556, June.

INCOMES DATA SERVICES (IDS) (1994c) *Sickness and Disability*. Employment Supplement No.71, August.

IDS (1998) *Managing Absence*. Study No.645. London, IDS.

IDS (1999), 'Dealing with persistent short-term absentees', *IDS Brief*, No 643, August. pp.12–17.

IDS (2001) *Attendance Matters*. Study No.702. London, IDS.

INDUSTRIAL RELATIONS SERVICES (IRS) (1994) 'Sickness absence monitoring and control: a survey of practice', *Industrial Relations Review and Report*, No.568, September. pp.4–16.

INDUSTRIAL RELATIONS SERVICES (1995) 'Sickness absence', *Industrial Relations Law Bulletin*, October. pp.2–9.

IRS (1998) 'Sickness absence: a survey of 182 employers', *IRS Employment Review: Employee Health Bulletin*, No 665, October. pp.2–20.

IRS (2000) 'Managing long-term absence', *IRS Employment Review: Employee Health Bulletin*, No.16, August. pp.3–12.

IRS (2001) 'Return-to-work policies and practices', *IRS Employment Review*, No.741, 3 December. pp.40–47.

Industrial Society (1994) *Managing Attendance*. London, Industrial Society.

Industrial Society (1997) *Managing Attendance*. London, Industrial Society.

Industrial Society (2001) *Maximising Attendance*. Managing Best Practice Report No.84. London, Industrial Society.

JAMES P., DIBBEN P. and CUNNINHAM I. (2000) 'Missing persons', *People Management*, Vol. 6, No.23, 23 November. pp.41–42.

JAMES P., CUNNINGHAM I. and DIBBEN P. (2001) 'Returning to work: employer policies and practices', *IRS Employment Trends: Employee Health Bulletin*, No.20, April. pp.12–14.

KORN A. (1999) 'The right reasons for ill health dismissal', *Personnel Today*, 10 June. p.18.

LABOUR RESEARCH DEPARTMENT (LRD) (1999) *Sickness Absence*

Policy: A trade unionist's guide. London, Labour Research Department Publications.

LEWIN K. (1951) *Field Theory in Social Science.* New York, Harper & Row.

LEWIS D. *and* SARGEANT M. (2000) *Essentials of Employment Law.* London, CIPD

MACDONALD L. (2001) *Managing Employee Absence.* Dublin, Blackhall.

MYLAND L. (2000) 'Case study: controlling absence', *Croner's Absence Briefing*, Issue No.9, 22 November. pp.2–3.

NICHOLSON N. (1977) 'Absence behaviour and attendance motivation: a conceptual synthesis', *Journal of Management Studies*, 14. pp.231–252.

RHODES S. R. *and* STEERS R. M. (1990) *Managing Employee Absenteeism.* Reading, Mass., Addison Wesley.

ROBBINS S. P. (1993) *Organisational Behaviour.* Englewood Cliffs, New Jersey, Prentice Hall.

ROETHLISBERGER F. J. *and* DICKSON W. J. (1939) *Management and the Worker.* Cambridge, Mass., Harvard University Press.

SCOTT K. D. *and* MARKHAM S. (1982) 'Absenteeism control methods: a survey of practices and results', *Personnel Administrator*, June. pp.73–84.

STAINES R. (2000) 'DfEE counts the cost of sick leave', *Personnel Today*, 28 November. p.12.

STEERS R. M. *and* RHODES S. R. (1978) 'Major influences on employee attendance: a process model', *Journal of Applied Psychology*, 63, 4. pp.391–407.

STEERS R. M. *and* RHODES S. R. (1984) 'Knowledge and speculation about absenteeism', in P. S. Goodman and R. S. Atkin (eds), *Absenteeism: New approaches to understanding, measuring and managing absence.* San Francisco, Jossey Bass.

SYRETT M. (1993) 'The best of everything', *Human Resources*, Winter. pp.83–86.

TAYLOR F. W. (1911) *The Principles of Scientific Management.* New York, Harper.

TRIST E. L., HIGGIN G. W., MURRAY H. *and* POLLOCK A. B. (1963) *Organisational Choice.* London, Tavistock.

WARR P. *and* YEARTA S. (1995) 'Health and motivational factors in sickness absence', *Human Resource Management Journal*, 5, 5. pp.33–48.

WICKENS P. (1987) *The Road to Nissan: Quality, flexibility and teamwork*. London, Macmillan.

INDEX